Dominic Bright is a barrister at Lamb Chambers, registered civil and commercial mediator with the Civil Mediation Council, and former judicial assistant to Sir Brian Leveson, then President of the Queen's Bench Division.

His recent articles include: 'The CICC and the Rule of Law: Fair, Transparent and Convenient? What You Need to Know about China's New International Commercial Court' (Counsel Magazine, September 2019); and 'Section 21 Sent Packing' (New Law Journal, 2 May 2019).

Dominic's forthcoming seminars include: 'Jurisdiction and Choice of Law Clauses in International Commercial Contracts' (November 2019); and 'Chattels, Fixtures, and Tenant's Improvements in Commercial Leases' (February 2020).

He is a member of the British Institute of International and Comparative Law, Property Bar Association, and Technology and Construction Bar Association.

For daily case digests, follow Dominic on LinkedIn and Twitter (LondonComBar).

A Practical Guide to the Small Claims Track

A Practical Guide to the Small Claims Track

Dominic Bright
Barrister, Lamb Chambers

Law Brief Publishing

© Dominic Bright

All rights reserved. No part of this publication may be reproduced, stored in a retrieval system, or transmitted, in any form or by any means, electronic, mechanical, photocopying, recording or otherwise, without the prior permission of the publisher.

Excerpts from judgments and statutes are Crown copyright. Any Crown Copyright material is reproduced with the permission of the Controller of OPSI and the Queen's Printer for Scotland. Some quotations may be licensed under the terms of the Open Government Licence (http://www.nationalarchives.gov.uk/doc/open-government-licence/version/3).

Cover image © iStockphoto.com/mammuth

The information in this book was believed to be correct at the time of writing. All content is for information purposes only and is not intended as legal advice. No liability is accepted by either the publisher or author for any errors or omissions (whether negligent or not) that it may contain. Professional advice should always be obtained before applying any information to particular circumstances.

Published 2019 by Law Brief Publishing, an imprint of Law Brief Publishing Ltd
30 The Parks
Minehead
Somerset
TA24 8BT

www.lawbriefpublishing.com

Paperback: 978-1-912687-45-9

For C.S. of Counsel.

FOREWORD

Over recent years, a succession of Lord Chancellors and Ministers of Justice have been keen to emphasise their commitment to protecting judges and upholding the rule of law. Such commitments are not without meaning and while the rule of law is a phrase often said, it is rarely examined. It is not an arid legal doctrine but is the foundation stone of much that creates a fair and just society.

It may be thought that the rule of law is of no relevance to a foreword about a book giving practical guidance to claims within the small claims track in the County Court. On the contrary, the rule of law is front and centre. It is because people with a dispute, however low in value and lacking complexity, can bring a claim before an impartial judge, that we can function as a civilised society where business can be done and wrongs remedied. The small claims procedure is a very real example of the rule of law in operation.

The District Bench across England and Wales is under pressure as it has never been before, with both the volume and variety of work that judges are obliged to hear. Added to that, judges generally, and the District Bench in particular, has to be able to reach both legal and factual decisions often without the benefit of the parties having legal representation. In order to fulfil their role properly and in order to continue with their duties to uphold the rule of law, without fear or favour, both full-time and deputy District Judges need to be able to manage heavy lists of both civil and family cases. A sizeable part of the daily diet of the District Bench will be civil claims which are allocated to the small claims track.

As Dominic Bright sets out, small claims account for approximately 60% of all allocations of civil work in the County Court and three-quarters of all civil claims disposed of by way of final hearing. The financial value of a small claim is now £10,000 or less and the track is designed to provide a proportionate procedure by which the most straightforward of these relatively low value claims can be decided without substantial pre-hearing preparation and without the formalities of a traditional trial. Of course, most people with a claim worth £10,000 or less are unlikely to consider the sums involved to be "small" and the title given to this track must not be seen to belittle the importance of the dispute to the parties involved. What is important is that the track provides a proportionate means of resolving a dispute between parties which can be of considerable practical importance and, despite the categorisation of small, considerable financial worth to the individuals involved.

In this comprehensive guide to the small claims track, Dominic Bright has set out all that a practitioner could possibly need to know about how to deal with a small claim, from allocation to judgment and through to any potential appeal. He covers the court's duty to manage cases actively and the overriding objective and, in doing so, points out the duty of the court to take into account the fact that a litigant is without representation when exercising powers of case management albeit that all rules, practice directions and orders apply equally to represented and unrepresented litigants. It is, of course, incumbent upon a practitioner, as well as the court, to act in furtherance of the overriding objective. An unrepresented litigant is not only entitled to a fair hearing, he is entitled to understand that he is obtaining that fair hearing.

Further to the specifics of how the court will deal with a small claim, including the pleadings, the allocation and the hearing itself, Dominic Bright has included guidance on a wide range of matters, such as ethics and ways to behave when in court, which will be of assistance to any junior practitioner appearing in a civil case at an early stage of their career. The inclusion of the civil procedure rules and practice directions relating to the small claims track, and also to pre-action conduct and protocols and to the overriding objective and the court's duty to manage cases, means that this guide provides a useful toolkit of relevant rules and practice directions.

This Practical Guide to the Small Claims Track will be of benefit to practitioners, particularly those new to practice. It will therefore be of benefit to the District Judges and their deputies who hear small claims. Undoubtedly, the better informed and prepared the representatives are, the better it is for the judges who hear such claims to enable them to concentrate on reaching the correct legal and factual conclusions in furtherance of upholding the rule of law.

HHJ Karen Walden-Smith
Senior Circuit Judge
Designated Civil Judge for
the County Court in East Anglia
November 2019

PREFACE

My aim is to shine light upon the 'what', 'when', and 'how' of the small claims track. This practical guide is written with junior *barristers* and *solicitors* in mind, however, *litigants in person* may also find it of some assistance. This is because the *special* procedure for dealing with these claims is designed so that *litigants* may conduct their *own* case.

It purports to be *clear*, *comprehensive*, and *concise*.

'Clear' because *short*, *descriptive* sub-headings are used to marshal content, often comprising just a few sentences; and sometimes, only one, *importance* sentence, containing a *single*, but *key* point.

'Comprehensive' because the full timeline of a claim is covered: from *pre-action*, through *final hearing*, to *appeal*. There are many, more comprehensive, authoritative texts on civil procedure in general, advocacy, and on the small claims track within the Intellectual Property Enterprise Court.

'Concise' because every effort has been made to remove jargon unencumbered with merit, unwarranted primary authority, and unnecessary secondary sources.

It aspires to be well-thumbed, throwing a beacon of light onto issues, *before*, and *when* they arise, so that they can be dealt with *confidently*, to the benefit of *lay* and *professional* clients, and enabling *the court* to achieve the overriding objective to deal with cases justly, and at proportionate cost.

The law in England and Wales is stated as at 1 November 2019.

Dominic Bright
Lamb Chambers, Temple, London
November 2019

"It is not the critic who counts; not the man who points out how the strong man stumbles or where the doer of deeds could have done them better. The credit belongs to the man who is actually in the arena, whose face is marred by dust and sweat and blood; who strives valiantly; who errs, who comes short again and again, because there is no effort without error and shortcoming; but who does actually strive to do the deeds; who knows great enthusiasms, the great devotions; who spends himself in a worthy cause; who at the best knows in the end the triumph of high achievement, and who at the worst, if he fails, at least fails while daring greatly, so that his place shall never be with those cold and timid souls who neither know victory nor defeat."

– Theodore Roosevelt
Sorbonne, Paris
April 1910

CONTENTS

1. **Overview**   1
   - a. Small claim   1
   - b. Context   2
   - c. Allocation   2
   - d. Civil Procedure Rules   3
   - e. Final remedy   3
   - f. Preparation   4
   - g. Experts   4
   - h. Preliminary hearing   5
   - i. Additional or amended directions   5
   - j. Final hearing   6
   - k. Non-attendance   6
   - l. Disposal without a hearing   7
   - m. Set aside & re-hearing   7
   - n. Costs   8
     - i. Pre-allocation   8
     - ii. After allocation   8
     - iii. Re-allocation   10

2. **Overriding objective**   11
   - a. Duty   11
     - i. Court   11
     - ii. Parties   11
   - b. Factors   12
     - i. Equal footing   12
       - 1. Litigants in person   13
       - 2. Correspondence   14
     - ii. Proportionality   15

3. Court's duty to actively manage cases	16
a. Encouraging co-operation	17
b. Early identification of issues	17
c. Summary disposal	18
d. Order of resolution	18
e. Alternative dispute resolution	19
f. Helping settlement	19
g. Controlling progress	19
h. Cost / benefit analysis	20
i. Efficiency	21
j. Directions	21
4. Pre-action protocols & Practice Direction – Pre-Action Conduct	22
a. Objectives	22
b. Reasonable & proportionate	22
c. Non-compliance	23
5. Statements of case	24
a. Types	24
b. Rules & practice directions	24
i. Legible & intelligible	25
ii. Heading	25
iii. Numbers & figures	25
iv. Authority & evidence	26
v. Particularity	26
vi. Contributory negligence	26
vii. Endorsement	27
viii. Statement of truth	27
1. Particulars of claim	27
2. Who	27
a. Legal representative	28

b. Companies & partnerships	28
c. Insurers	28
3. Default	29

6. Claim form — 30

a. Substantial dispute of fact	30
b. Court	30
c. Parties	31
i. Individuals	31
ii. Companies & partnerships	31
iii. Insurers	31
d. Address	32
i. Individuals	32
ii. Businesses	32
e. Detail	32
f. Value	33
g. Interest	33
h. Preferred hearing centre	33
i. Individual	33
ii. Not an individual	33
iii. Transfer	34
i. Address for service	34
i. Claimant	34
ii. Defendant	35
j. Fees & costs	35
k. Remission	35
l. Issue	35

7. Particulars of claim — 37

a. Within claim form or separate document	37
b. Contents	37
c. Breach of contract	38

i. Written	38
ii. Oral	38
iii. Conduct	38
d. Personal injury	39
e. Statement of facts	39
f. Considerations following a road traffic collision	40
i. When, where & who	40
ii. Road layout	40
iii. Traffic	40
iv. Weather	41
v. Vehicles	41
vi. Speed	41
vii. Proximity	41
viii. Perception	41
ix. Objective intention	42
x. Subjective intention	42
xi. Mechanism	42
xii. Mitigation	42
xiii. Damage	43
g. Interest	43
i. Contractual	43
ii. Statutory	44
1. County Courts Act 1984	44
2. Late Payment of Commercial Debts (Interest) Act 1998	44
iii. Personal injury	45
8. Defence (& counterclaim)	**46**
a. Response	46
b. Address for service	47
c. Individuals	47
d. Counterclaim	47

9. Reply to the defence (& counterclaim)	49
a. Reply	49
b. Defence	49
10. Directions questionnaires	50
a. Notice of proposed allocation	50
b. Filing	50
c. Default	51
d. Informing the court	51
e. Small Claims Mediation Service	52
f. Stay	53
g. Track	53
h. Hearing centre	53
i. Experts	54
j. Witnesses	55
k. Interpreters	55
l. Signature	56
m. Further information	56
n. Other directions	57
11. Allocation	58
a. Generally suitable	58
b. Relevant matters	58
i. Financial value	59
1. Amount in dispute	59
2. Admissions	60
3. Zero	60
ii. Remedy	61
iii. Factual, legal or evidential complexity	61
iv. Counterclaim / Part 20 claim	61
v. Oral evidence	61
vi. Party view	62

    c. Pre-allocation hearing   62
    d. Challenging   62
    e. Standard directions   63
    f. Witness statements   64
    g. Experts   64
    h. Special directions   65
    i. Preliminary hearing   67
    j. Hearing fee   68
    k. Disposal without a hearing   68

12. **Preparation**   69
    a. Contact   69
    b. Scan   70
        i. Instructions   70
            1. Enclosures   71
            2. Clients   71
            3. Facts   71
            4. Issues   72
            5. Authority   72
            6. Costs   72
            7. Offers   73
            8. Interim payments   73
            9. Contact details   73
        ii. Statements of case   74
            1. Compliant   74
            2. Names   74
        iii. Evidence   74
            1. In the papers   75
            2. Not in the papers   76
        iv. Orders   76
        v. Correspondence   77
            1. Pre-action   77

2. Filing & service	77
3. Offers	77
4. Interim payments	78
c. Analyse	78
i. Agreed facts	78
ii. Disputed facts	79
iii. Issues	80
d. Checklist of information & documents	80
i. Road traffic	80
ii. Building, repairs, goods sold & contract	81
iii. Landlord & tenant	81
iv. Breach of duty	81
e. Telephone	81
f. Spare copies	82
13. Authority	**83**
a. Legal principle	83
b. Practice Direction (Citation of Authorities) [2012] 1 WLR 780	84
i. Official Law Reports	84
ii. Weekly Law Reports & All England Law Reports	84
iii. Specialist series	84
iv. Other reports	85
v. Transcripts	85
vi. Format	85
c. Practice Direction (Citation of Authorities) [2001] 1 WLR 1001	85
i. Relevant & useful	86
ii. Adverse authority	86
iii. County court authority	87
d. Citation	87
e. Marked	87

f. Spare copies	88
g. Cost / benefit	88
h. Context	89
i. Subsequent consideration	89
ii. Determined appeal	89
iii. Pending appeal	90
14. Skeleton arguments	92
a. Assist the court	92
b. Requirements	92
i. Concision	93
1. Headings & sub-headings	93
2. Lists & punctuation	93
3. Layout	94
ii. Define & confine areas of controversy	94
iii. Numbering	94
iv. Cross-referencing	94
v. Self-contained	96
vi. Quotations	96
c. Content	96
i. Headings	96
ii. Reading time	97
iii. Invitation	97
iv. Facts	97
v. Costs	99
vi. Sign & date	99
vii. Back sheet	99
viii. Spelling, grammar & punctuation	100
d. Form	100
e. Notice	100
i. File & serve	101
ii. Springboard	101

15. **Arrival**	102
a. Sign in	102
b. Note	102
c. Listing	103
i. Managing expectations	103
ii. Spare copies	104
iii. County Court at Central London	104
iv. Alternative dispute resolution	104
v. Subsequent listing	105
d. Non-attendance of witnesses	105
e. Late attendance of legal representative	106
f. Conference	107
g. Speak to the other party	107
i. Papers	107
ii. Issues	108
iii. Quantum	108
iv. Authority	109
v. Costs, disbursements & witness expenses	109
h. Case management form	109
16. **Conference**	111
a. Build rapport	111
i. Greeting	111
ii. Privacy	112
iii. Break the ice	112
iv. Note	112
b. Outline the procedure	113
i. Before	113
ii. During	113
1. Entering & exiting court	113
2. Giving evidence	114
3. Submissions & judgment	114

  iii. After   115
 c. Questioning   115
  i. Ethics   115
  ii. Active listening   115
  iii. English   116
  iv. Confirm written evidence   117
  v. Fill in any gaps   117
  vi. Loss of earnings & expenses   118
 d. Advising   118
 e. Time management   118

17. **Applications**   119
 a. Default judgment   119
  i. Administrative   120
  ii. Excluded claims   120
  iii. Default of acknowledgement of service   120
  iv. Default of defence   120
  v. Procedure   121
  vi. Set aside   121
 b. Transfer   122
 c. Consent   122
 d. Summary judgment   122
  i. When   123
  ii. Allocation hearing   123
  iii. Grounds   123
 e. Strike out   124
  i. When   124
  ii. Grounds   124
   1. No reasonable grounds   125
   2. Abuse of process & obstructing just disposal   125
   3. Default   126
    a. Statement of truth   126

b. Unless order	126
c. Inability to read or sign	126
f. Adjourn	127
i. Overriding objective	128
ii. Health	128
g. Set aside	129
h. Relief from sanctions	130
i. Need	130
ii. Evidence	131
iii. Three-stage test	131
1. Seriousness & significance	131
2. Reason	132
3. All the circumstances	133
a. Proportionality	133
b. Compliance	134
c. Promptness	134
d. Opportunism	134
18. Procedure of the final hearing	136
a. Judge	136
b. Representation	136
c. Public	137
d. Recording	138
i. Official	138
ii. Unofficial	138
1. Contempt of Court Act 1981	138
2. Practice Direction (Tape Recorders) [1981] 1 WLR 1526	139
3. Sentence	139
e. Evidence	140
f. Cross-examination	140
g. Judicial intervention v entering the arena	141

i. Judicial intervention	141
ii. Entering the arena	142
1. Fairness	142
2. Guidance	143

19. Witness evidence — 145

a. Contemporaneous	145
b. Statements	146
i. Formalities	147
ii. Form	147
iii. Statement of truth	148
iv. Inability to read or sign	148
v. Contemporaneous	149
vi. Detail	149
vii. Hearsay notice	150
viii. Non-attendance	151
1. Factors	151
2. Practice	152
c. Oral	152
i. Application to decide in absence	153
ii. Claimant	154
iii. Defendant	154
iv. Claimant & defendant	154

20. Independent & objective evidence — 155

a. Witnesses	155
b. Photographs	155
i. Clear	156
ii. Location	156
iii. Road layout	156
iv. Damage	157
c. Sketch plans	157

d. Engineers' reports	157
i. Collision	158
ii. Impact	158
iii. Damage	158
iv. Value	158
v. Write-off	159
vi. Roadworthy	159
vii. Pictures	159
e. The Highway Code	160
f. Judicial College Guidelines	161
21. Submissions	162
a. Opening	162
b. Closing	162
i. Order	162
ii. Approach to fact-finding	163
iii. Credibility	165
1. Agreed facts	166
2. Internal inconsistency	166
3. Consistent previous statements	167
iv. Inherent unlikelihood	168
22. Orders & judgment	169
a. Orders	169
i. Carriage	169
ii. Consent	170
iii. Tomlin	170
iv. Unless	171
b. Judgment	171
i. Default	171
ii. After final hearing	171
1. Ex tempore	172

2. Reserved	172
iii. Slip rule	172
iv. Reasons	173
1. Duty	173
2. Note	175
3. Failure	175
v. Reconsideration	175
vi. Appeals	177
1. Note	177
2. Signed copy	177
c. Time limits for compliance	177
23. Costs, disbursements & witness expenses	**178**
a. General discretion	178
i. Payable	178
1. Conduct	179
2. Limited success	179
3. Offers	180
ii. Amount	180
iii. When	180
b. Fees	180
i. Issue	181
ii. Hearing	182
iii. Application	182
1. On notice	182
2. Consent	182
3. Permission to appeal	183
iv. Remission	183
c. Legal representatives	183
i. Specified sum	183
ii. Unspecified sum	184
iii. Counterclaim	185

iv. Injunction	185
d. Party or witness	185
i. Loss of earnings	185
1. Employed	185
2. Self-employed	186
3. Other	186
ii. Travel expenses	186
1. Reasonable	187
2. Purpose	187
e. Expert	187
f. Lay representative	187
g. Personal injury	188
h. Appeal	188
i. Re-allocation	188
i. After leaving the small claims track	188
ii. Before re-allocation to the small claims track	189
24. Unreasonable behaviour	**190**
a. Disapplication of fixed costs	190
b. Definition	190
i. Authority	190
1. Behaved unreasonably	190
2. Unreasonable	192
3. Unreasonable conduct	193
ii. Statutory construction	194
c. Relevant circumstances	195
i. Pre-action protocols & Practice Direction – Pre-Action Conduct	196
ii. Non-compliance	196
iii. Evidence	196
iv. Issues raised, pursued or contested	197
1. Abuse of process	197

2. Summary judgment	198
a. Represented	198
b. Unrepresented	198
3. Manner in which a case is pursued	199
a. Offers	199
b. Non-attendance	199
i. Party	200
ii. Witness	200
4. Exaggeration	201
5. Unnecessary applications	201
6. Communications	202
7. Opportunism	203
d. Summary assessment	203
e. Statement of costs	203
i. Particulars	204
1. Grade & number of hours	204
2. Rate	204
a. London	206
b. National	206
ii. Notice	207
iii. Absence	207
25. Appeals	208
a. Court	208
b. Centre	208
c. Permission	209
i. Need	209
ii. Test	209
1. First appeal	209
2. Second appeal	210
iii. Oral application	211
iv. Appellant's notice	211

1. Fee	211
2. Documents	212
3. Grounds	212
4. Transcript	212
v. Respondent's notice	212
1. Permission	213
2. Service	213
d. Skeleton arguments	213
e. Appeal bundle	214
i. Relevant	214
ii. May be relevant	215
iii. Service	215
iv. Respondent's documents	215
f. Applications	216
i. Stay	216
ii. Extension	216
g. Determination	216
h. Costs	217
26. Attendance notes	218
a. Utility	218
i. Counsel	218
ii. Professional client	219
iii. Lay client	219
b. Fundamentals	220
c. Outcome	220
d. Correspondence	221
i. Professional client	221
ii. Lay client	221
iii. Other party	222
e. Tactical & strategic decisions	222
f. Additional instructions	223

g. During hearing	223
i. Shorthand	223
ii. Evidence	224
iii. Submissions	225
iv. Judgment	225
v. Order	226
h. Next steps	226
i. Travel expenses	226
j. Contact details	227
k. Telephone	227
l. Email	227
27. Tools	229
a. Smart phone	229
b. Laptop	230
i. Hardware	230
ii. Software	230
c. Online resources	231
d. Notepad	231
e. Disk drive	232
f. Tablet	233
g. The Highway Code	233
h. Judicial College Guidelines	233
i. Props	233
j. External encrypted vault	234
28. Dress	235
29. Ethics	236
a. Confidants	236
b. Ethical Enquiries Services	237

30. Etiquette	238
a. Outside court	238
i. Punctuality	238
ii. Coats, umbrellas & bags	239
iii. Disposal	239
iv. Correspondence	240
1. Judge	240
2. Ushers & other court staff	240
3. Professional client	241
4. Practice manager	241
b. Inside court	241
i. Mobile telephones	242
ii. Entering & exiting	242
iii. Seating	243
1. Parties	243
2. Witnesses	244
3. Non-court actors	244
iv. Submissions	244
1. Forms of address	245
2. Introduction	245
3. Interrupting	246
4. Humility	246
5. Gestures	246
6. Criticism	247
a. Experts	247
b. Legal representatives	247
Annex A: CPR 1.1 — The Overriding Objective	249
Annex B: CPR 1.4 — Court's Duty To Manage Cases	250
Annex C: Part 27 — The Small Claims Track	252

Annex D: Practice Direction 27 — Small Claims Track   263

Annex E: Practice Direction — Pre-Action Conduct   273
                          and Protocols

1. Overview

This chapter provides an overview of the special procedure for dealing with claims that have been allocated to the small claims track (see appendices C and D). Specific reference is made only to those that are of *fundamental* importance. The remaining chapters go further, providing *guidance* as to when to rely upon *specific* rules, and *when* to deploy authority interpreting them.

a. Small claim

The rules of civil litigation in England and Wales are prescribed in the Civil Procedure Rules ("CPR"). Part 27 of the CPR is entitled: 'The small claims track'. A 'small claim' is a claim that falls under this Part which (CPR 27.1(1)): 1) sets out the procedure for dealing with small claims; and 2) limits the amount of costs that can be recovered.

The special procedure for dealing with claims that have been allocated to the small claims track 'is intended to provide a proportionate procedure by which most straightforward claims with a financial value of not more than £10,000 can be decided, without the need for substantial pre-hearing preparation and the formalities of a traditional trial, and without incurring large legal costs' (Practice Direction ("PD") 26 at [8.1(1)(a)]).

There are at least three reasons why it is, perhaps, regrettable that claims that have been allocated to the small claims track are referred to as "small claims".

First, they make up about *three quarters* of all civil claims disposed of by way of final hearing. Secondly, many would not accept that *£10,000* is a "small" sum. Thirdly, the claimant bringing the claim, and the defendant defending against it, are both likely to disagree that the importance of their dispute is "small".

b. Context

In April to June 2019, 25,000 cases were allocated to the small claims track. This is just shy of 60 percent of all allocations (to any track). Of the claims that went to trial, about three quarters were allocated to the small claims track – a two percent increase when compared to the same quarter in the previous year. The average time that a claim allocated to the small claims track takes to go to a final hearing is about 37 weeks (Ministry of Justice, *Civil Justice Statistics Quarterly, England and Wales, April to June 2019 (provisional)*, 5 September 2019).

c. Allocation

The small claims track is the 'normal track' for three types of claim (CPRs 26.6 and 27.1(2)).

First, any claim which has a value of not more than £10,000. In practice, this type of claim forms the overwhelming majority of claims that are allocated to the small claims track.

Secondly, a 'claim for personal injuries' where: 1) the value of the claim is not more than £10,000; and 2) the value of any claim for 'damages for personal injuries' is not more than £1,000. A 'claim for personal injuries' is one in which 'there is a claim for damages in respect of personal injuries to the claimant or any other person or in respect of a person's death'. 'Damages in respect of personal injuries' means 'damages claimed as compensation for pain, suffering and loss of amenity and does not include any other damages which are claimed'.

Thirdly, any claim which includes a claim by a tenant of residential premises against a landlord where: 1) the tenant is seeking an order requiring the landlord to carry out repairs, or other work to the premises; and 2) the cost of the repairs, or other work, to the premises is estimated to be not more than £1,000. If a tenant of residential premises is claiming a remedy in respect of harassment, or unlawful eviction, it will *not* be allocated to the small claims track.

d. Civil Procedure Rules

CPRs and PDs apply to small claims, except to the extent that the CPRs and PDs provide otherwise. CPRs relating to the following do not apply (CPR 27.2):

1. interim remedies (except as it relates to interim injunctions);
2. disclosure and inspection;
3. evidence (except the power of the court to control evidence);
4. miscellaneous rules about evidence;
5. experts and assessors (except the duty to restrict expert evidence; experts' overriding duty to the court; the court's power to direct that evidence is to be given by a single joint expert; and instructions to a single joint expert);
6. further information (although the court may, on the court's own motion, order a party to provide further information if the court considers that it is appropriate);
7. Part 36 offers to settle; and
8. hearings (except the general rule that hearings are public; and regarding communications with the court).

e. Final remedy

The court may grant any final remedy in relation to a small claim which it could grant if the proceedings were allocated to the fast track, or to the multi-track (CPR 27.3).

f. Preparation

After allocation, the court will do one of the following three (CPR 27.4).

First, give *standard* directions, and fix a date for the final hearing. Secondly, give *special* directions, and fix a date for the final hearing, or direct that the court consider what further directions are to be given, no later than 28 days after the date that special directions were given.

Thirdly, fix a date for a *preliminary* hearing. Fourthly, give notice that the court proposes to deal with the claim *without* a hearing, inviting the parties to notify the court by a specified date if they agree.

'Standard directions' means: 1) 'a direction that each party shall, at least 14 days before the date fixed for the final hearing, file and serve on every other party copies of all documents (including any expert's report) on which she intends to rely at the hearing'; and 2) any other standard directions prescribed in PD 27.

'Special directions' means 'directions given in addition to or instead of the standard directions.'

The general rule is that the court will give the parties at least 21 days' notice of the date fixed for the final hearing. The exception is where the parties agree to accept less notice. In any event, the court must inform the parties of the amount of time allowed for the final hearing.

g. Experts

No expert evidence may be given at a hearing without the court's permission (CPR 27.5).

h. Preliminary hearing

A preliminary hearing may only be held in three circumstances (CPR 27.6).

First, special directions are needed to ensure a fair hearing, and it appears to the court that it is necessary for a party to attend at court to ensure that she *understands what she must do* to comply with the special directions. Secondly, to be able to *dispose of the claim*, on the basis that one of the parties has no real prospect of success at a final hearing. Thirdly, to enable the court to *strike out a statement of case*, or part thereof, on the basis that it discloses no reasonable grounds for bringing, or of defending the claim.

When deciding whether or not to hold a preliminary hearing, the court must have regard to the desirability of *limiting the expense of the parties* that will be incurred in them having to attend court. The parties must be given at least 14 days' notice of the date of such a hearing.

If all the *parties agree*, the court may treat the *preliminary* hearing as a *final* hearing.

At, or after a preliminary hearing, the court will do three things.

First, fix the date of the final hearing (if the court has not so fixed already), and give the parties at least 21 days' notice of the same, unless the parties agree to accept less notice. Secondly, inform the parties of the amount of time allowed for the final hearing. Thirdly, give appropriate directions.

i. Additional or amended directions

The court may add to, vary, or revoke, directions (CPR 27.7).

j. Final hearing

There are six main rules for the final hearing (CPR 27.8).

First, the court may adopt *any* method of proceeding that it considers to be *fair*. Secondly, hearings will be *informal*. Thirdly, the *strict* rules of evidence do *not* apply. Fourthly, evidence need *not* be on oath. Fifthly, the court may *limit* cross-examination. Sixthly, the court *must* give reasons for its decision.

k. Non-attendance

If a party who does not attend the final hearing satisfies the following three criteria, the court will take into account that party's statement of case, and any other documents that she has filed when the claim is decided (CPR 27.9).

First, at least seven days before the hearing, written notice ("notice") that she will not attend has been filed with the court and served on the other party. Secondly, at least seven days before the hearing, she has served any other documents on the other party which she has filed with the court. Thirdly, in her written notice, she has requested that the court decide the claim in her absence, and she has confirmed her compliance with the first and second criteria.

Otherwise, the court may strike out the claim (CPR 27.9(2)).

The court may decide the claim solely on the evidence of the claimant if two conditions are satisfied (CPR 27.9(3)). Firstly, a defendant does not attend the hearing, or give notice. Secondly, the claimant does not attend the hearing, or gives notice that she will not attend.

The court may *strike out* a claim, defence, and counterclaim if *neither party attends, nor* gives *notice* (CPR 27.9(4)).

l. Disposal without a hearing

If all parties agree, the court may deal with a claim without a hearing (CPR 27.10).

m. Set aside & re-hearing

Where three conditions are met, a party may apply for an order that judgment is set aside, and that the claim is re-heard (CPR 27.11).

First, she was neither present, nor represented, at the hearing of the claim. Secondly, she has not given notice to the court, in accordance with the rule for non-attendance at the final hearing (see above). Thirdly, the application must be made not more than 14 days after the day on which notice of the judgment was served on her.

Where these conditions are satisfied, a court may grant an application, but only if the applicant satisfies a further two conditions. First, she had a good reason for not attending, or being represented at the hearing, or giving notice to the court, in accordance with the rule for non-attendance at a final hearing. Secondly, she has a reasonable prospect of success.

If a judgment is set aside, the court must fix a new date for the hearing of the claim. The hearing may take place immediately after the set aside application. It may also be heard by the judge who granted the application.

An application to set aside cannot succeed where the claim was disposed of without a hearing.

n. Costs

There are three overarching rules governing costs of a claim that is allocated to the small claims track. First, pre-allocation. Secondly, after allocation. Thirdly, re-allocation.

i. Pre-allocation

CPRs 46.11 and 46.13 prescribe the rules for costs before a claim has been allocated to the small claims track (CPR 27.14(1)). In general, once a claim is allocated to the small claims track, the rules that apply to costs on the small claims track apply to the period *before* the claim was allocated to the small claims track, as well as *after* (CPR 46.11). The exception is where the court, or a practice direction, provides otherwise.

Any cost orders made *before* a claim is allocated to the small claims track will *not* be affected by allocation. In general, where a claim is allocated to the small claims track, and the court subsequently re-allocates the claim to a different track, any special rules about costs applying: 1) to the first track, apply *up to* the date of reallocation; and 2) to the second track, apply *from* the date of reallocation. The exception is where the court orders otherwise (CPR 46.13(2)).

Where a case settles before allocation, for example, and assessment of costs is on the standard basis, the court may restrict costs to those that would have been allowed on the small claims track, if the claim would in fact have been so allocated (CPR 46.13(3)).

ii. After allocation

The only sum that one party ("A") can be ordered to pay to another party ("B"), in respect of B's costs, fees, and expenses, including those relating to an appeal (CPR 27.14 and PD 27 at [7.3]) are:

1. fixed costs, attributable to issuing the claim, which

a) are payable under the rule prescribing fixed costs (CPR 45) or,
   b) would be payable under CPR 45 if it applied to the claim;
2. in proceedings which included a claim for an injunction, or an order for specific performance of a sum not exceeding the amount specified in PD 27 for legal advice, and assistance relating to that claim;
3. any court fees paid by that other party;
4. expenses which a party, or witness has reasonably incurred in travelling to, and from, a hearing, or staying away from home for the purpose of attending a hearing;
5. a sum not exceeding £95 for any loss of earnings, or loss of leave by a party, or witness, due to attending a hearing, or staying away from home for the purpose of attending a hearing;
6. a sum not exceeding £750 for an expert's fees;
7. such further costs as the court may assess by the summary procedure, and order to be paid by a party who has 'behaved unreasonably';
8. Stage 1, and, where relevant, Stage 2 fixed costs, under CPR 45.18, where
   a) the claim was within the scope of the Pre-Action Protocol for Low Value Personal Injury Claims in Road Traffic Accidents, or the Pre-Action Protocol for Low Value Personal Injury (Employers' Liability and Public Liability) Claims,
   b) the claimant reasonably believed that the claim was valued at more than the small claims track limit, in accordance with the relevant protocol, and
   c) the defendant did not pay those Stage 1, and, where relevant, Stage 2 fixed costs; and
9. in an appeal, the cost of any approved transcript that was reasonably incurred.

'Behaved unreasonably' does not necessarily include a party who has rejected an offer in settlement, but the court may take this into consideration.

The limits on costs also apply to any fee, or reward, charged by a person exercising rights of audience as a lay representative for acting on behalf of a party to proceedings.

iii. Re-allocation

Where a claim is allocated to the small claims track, and subsequently re-allocated to another track, the rule prescribing costs on the small claims track will *cease* to apply *after* the claim has been *re*-allocated (CPR 27.15). Fast track or multi-track costs will apply from the date of re-allocation.

2. Overriding objective

The overriding objective of civil litigation is to enable the court to deal with cases *justly*, and at *proportionate cost* (CPR 1.1(1) and appendix A). This includes six *factors*, of which one is dealing with the case in ways that are proportionate. This, in turn, has four *aspects*. To further the overriding objective, the court must *actively manage cases*, which includes 12 *considerations*.

Whenever any application is heard, case management decision is made, or judgment is given, the following factors can be deployed effectively in any case that has been allocated to the small claims track. When used as the bones on which the flesh of a submission is based, they can be simple, persuasive, and *decisive*.

a. Duty

The CPR imposes *different* duties on the *court* and the *parties*.

i. Court

The *court* must seek to give effect to the overriding objective when exercising any power or interpreting any rule (CPR 1.2). This includes actively managing cases, so as to further the overriding objective (CPR 1.4(1)).

ii. Parties

The *parties* must help the court to further the overriding objective (CPR 1.3).

This duty to help the *court* is not a duty to help *another party*. There is no duty on one party ("A") to assist another party ("B") to remedy a procedural mistake made by B, unless there is a *genuine* misunderstanding, relating to a *material* matter, to which A has *contributed*.

A is entitled to take a good procedural point, but in doing so, A should act "in a proper professional manner in researching the position, advising the client and taking their instructions", so that it cannot be recast as "technical games" (*Woodward & Anor v Phoenix Healthcare Distribution Ltd* [2019] EWCA Civ 985 at [50]).

b. Factors

Dealing with a case justly and at proportionate cost includes giving consideration to six factors (CPR 1.1(2)). They are *not* exhaustive, which is clear from the word 'includes'. They are *not* expressed to be hierarchical. *Neither* are they absolute requirements, which is demonstrated by the qualification that dealing with a case justly and at proportionate cost includes the six factors, 'so far as is practicable'.

First, ensuring that parties are on an equal footing. Secondly, saving expense. Thirdly, ensuring that the case is dealt with expeditiously and fairly.

Fourthly, allotting an appropriate share of the court's resources to the case, while taking into account the need to allot resources to other cases. Fifthly, enforcing compliance with rules, practice directions, and court orders. Sixthly, dealing with the case in ways which are proportionate, of which there are four aspects (see below).

i. Equal footing

There are two important ways in which the parties should be on an equal footing in a claim that is allocated to the small claims track.

First, recognising that unrepresented litigants may justify such procedure at any hearing as the court considers appropriate to further the overriding objective. Secondly, procedural and substantive correspondence with the court should be served on the other side.

1. Litigants in person

Where a party is unrepresented, the court *must* have regard to this fact when *exercising any power of case management*. The court must adopt such procedure at any hearing as it considers appropriate to further the overriding objective, including the following.

First, ascertaining from an unrepresented party the matters about which the witness may be able to give evidence, or ought to be cross-examined. Secondly, putting, or causing to be put, to the witness such questions as may appear to the court to be proper (CPR 3.1A).

This does *not* lower the standard of compliance with rules, practice directions, or court orders. In practice, it usually means that, when making *case management directions*, they should be clear, understandable, and achievable, to unrepresented litigants. Rules, practice directions, and court orders apply to *all* litigants, *regardless* of whether or not they are represented.

This is clear from the recent decision of the Supreme Court in *Barton v Wright Hassal LLP* [2018] UKSC 12, [2018] 3 All ER 487 at [18], where Lord Sumption (with whom Lords Wilson and Carnwath agreed) said (with emphasis added):

> "… lack of representation will often justify making allowances in making *case management decisions* and in conducting hearings. But *it will not usually justify applying to litigants in person a lower standard of compliance with rules or orders of the court*. The overriding objective requires the courts so far as practicable to enforce compliance with the rules: CPR rule 1.1(1)(f). *The rules do not in any relevant respect distinguish between represented and unrepresented parties*.… Unless the rules and practice directions are *particularly inaccessible or obscure*, it is reasonable to expect a lit-

igant in person to familiarise himself with the rules which apply to any step which he is about to take."

Lord Briggs (with whom the President of the Supreme Court agreed) said (with emphasis added) at paragraph 42:

"… Save to the very limited extent to which the CPR now provides otherwise, *there cannot fairly be one attitude to compliance with rules for represented parties and another for litigants in person*, still less a general dispensation for the latter from the need to observe them. …"

The court must approach non-compliance by *un*represented parties, then, in the *same* way that it would approach non-compliance by *represented* parties. Failure to do so is an unjustifiable disturbance in the balance struck by the CPRs.

The exception to which Lord Sumption referred does *not* carve out a general exception for claims that have been allocated to the small claims track. The rules and practice directions that are applicable to the small claims track are, *by definition*, unlikely to be particularly inaccessible or obscure.

2. Correspondence

As a general rule, *any* communication with the *court* on a matter of *substance* or *procedure* must be *disclosed* to, and served on, the other party (CPRs 27.2(1)(h) and 39.8). Failure to do so, so as to deprive the other party of an opportunity to respond, amounts to "a serious procedural irregularity" (*National Westminster Bank Plc v Rushmer* [2010] EWHC 554 (Ch), [2010] 2 FLR 362 at [35]).

ii. Proportionality

Consideration should be given to four aspects of a case, so as to ensure that it is dealt with in ways that are proportionate (CPR 1.1(2)(c)).

First, the amount of *money* involved. Secondly, the *importance* of the case. Thirdly, the *complexity* of the issues. Fourthly, the *financial position* of each party.

3. Court's duty to actively manage cases

The court must actively manage cases, so as to further the overriding objective (CPR 1.4(1) and appendix B). There are 12 considerations that are expressly included in active case management. They are *not* exhaustive. *Neither* are they expressed to be hierarchical.

They can be deployed whenever the court has to exercise a discretion, so as to persuade the court that, the way in which you invite the court to exercise a discretion is in accordance with the duty to *actively manage cases*, and, therefore, the *overriding objective*, which the court *must* seek to further.

First, *encouraging parties to co-operate* with each other in the conduct of proceedings. Secondly, *identifying the issues* at an early stage. Thirdly, deciding promptly which issues need full investigation, followed by a final hearing, and *disposing summarily* of those that do not. Fourthly, *deciding the order* in which issues are to be resolved. Fifthly, encouraging the parties to use *alternative dispute resolution*, if appropriate, and *facilitating* the same.

Sixthly, *helping the parties to settle* the whole, or part of the case. Seventhly, *fixing timetables*, or otherwise controlling the progress of the case. Eighthly, considering whether the *likely benefits* of taking a particular step justify the *cost* of taking it. Ninthly, dealing with as many aspects of the case as it can on the *same* occasion. Tenthly, dealing with the case *without* parties needing to attend court in person. Eleventhly, making use of *technology*. Twelfthly, giving directions to ensure that the trial of a case proceeds, both *quickly*, and *efficiently*.

a. Encouraging co-operation

Where there is no pre-action letter, a party fails to reply to sustained correspondence over a prolonged period, or unreasonably refuses to consider an offer of alternative dispute resolution, the court *should* act accordingly.

Failure to do so is incompatible with the court's duty to actively manage cases, so as to further the overriding objective, which the parties are obliged to help the court to achieve. These arguments can, perhaps, be best deployed in an application for costs on the basis that a party has behaved unreasonably.

b. Early identification of issues

The *key* documents relevant to the issues in dispute should be disclosed *before* a claim is issued (PD – Pre-Action Conduct and Protocols at [6(c)]). Particulars of claim must set out the claim in a clear, coherent, way, that conforms to practice directions (CPR 16.4(1)(e)). In a claim based upon a written agreement, this includes *attaching* a copy of the contract (or documents constituting the agreement) to the particulars of claim, or *service with* the particulars of claim (PD 16 at [7.3]).

Where a party ("A") fails to do so, an application should be made by the innocent party ("B") – inviting the court to exercise its case management powers – to strike out A's statement of case, on the basis of A's *material* failures to comply with the rules and practice directions (CPR 3.4(2)(c)). The submission is that: the *court* is under a *duty* actively to manage the case; the issues have *not* been identified at an early stage; so that the *court* has been *un*able to further the overriding objective to deal with the case *justly* and *proportionately*, which includes *enforcing compliance* with rules and practice directions.

c. Summary disposal

Where *particulars of claim* disclose no reasonable grounds for *bringing* a claim, or a *defence* discloses no reasonable grounds for *defending* against a claim, an application should be made – inviting the court to exercise its case management powers – to strike out that statement of case and / or for summary judgment (CPRs 3.4(2)(a) and 24.2).

The issues in these statements of case do *not* need a final hearing, or even full investigation. If allowed to proceed, they would be *bound to fail*, the case would *not* be dealt with *expeditiously*, and an *inappropriate* share of the court's resources would have been allocated to the case. It follows that *summary* disposal is *appropriate*, and that it is *required* by the overriding objective.

In a claim for credit hire, for example, if there is no evidence of *basic* hire rates, it is hard to foresee a need to cross-examine, so as to establish whether or not the claimant is impecunious. This is because, *regardless* of whether or not the claimant is found to be impecunious, the court will likely award the *credit* hire rate, as there is *no* alternative evidence (of the *basic* hire rate).

As it is *un*likely to have *any* effect on judgment, there may be no *need* to resolve the "issue" of impecuniosity. Accordingly, the defendant may accept that the claimant is impecunious, so that this issue falls away, court time is saved, and that the case is dealt with expeditiously.

d. Order of resolution

The obvious example is that liability should be resolved before quantum. If liability is not established, it is unnecessary to resolve the issue of quantum.

In the credit hire example, where disputed, whether or not there was a need to hire should be resolved first. This is because, if there was no need to hire, the claim should be dismissed, so that the question of quantum becomes academic.

e. Alternative dispute resolution

All parties must agree before the case can be referred to the Small Claims Mediation Service.

This is why section A1 of the directions questionnaire is so important, enquiring whether a party agrees to the claim being referred to the Small Claims Mediation Service. The directions questionnaire must be completed and filed with the court. Upon receipt, and upon the request of the parties, the court will stay proceedings for one month (CPR 26.4(2)).

f. Helping settlement

On the day of the final hearing, where the parties consider that there is a *real* prospect of *settling* the claim, or even *narrowing the issues*, the court should give an *appropriate* amount of time to enable the parties to do so. Of course, this is in accordance with the overriding objective, to allot an appropriate share of the court's resources to the case, while taking into account the need to allot resources to other cases.

g. Controlling progress

Where a statement of case does not have a statement of truth, for example, the court should make an 'unless' order. That is, unless that statement of case is verified by a statement of truth, which is then filed and served before a certain date, it will automatically be struck out (PD 22 at [4.2]).

This is an example of the *court* fulfilling the *duty* to actively manage cases, through fixing a timetable, so as to control the progress of the case, without *waiting* for a *party* having to make (and pay the issue fee for) an application. In this way, the *court* ensures that a case progresses, even if the *parties* fail to do so.

h. Cost / benefit analysis

Where the claimant fails to attend a final hearing without giving notice, or a good reason for failing to attend, the court should consider whether the likely benefits of adjourning the case justify doing so. Where the amount in dispute is modest, and counsel for both sides have attended, the court will weigh up the following.

The unfairness to the defendant occasioned by granting an adjournment, including: the expense of attending that hearing; the additional expense of attending a further hearing; and that the case is not being dealt with expeditiously.

Balanced against this, the court will weigh any unfairness to the claimant if an adjournment is not granted: the defendant may have already admitted liability; the case may be of significant importance for the claimant; and the financial circumstances of the claimant may be dire (she might be an impecunious individual, as opposed to an affluent insurer).

Also, the court will factor in the need to allot an appropriate share of the court's resources to the case, while taking into account the need to allot resources to other cases.

i. Efficiency

Special directions may be needed to ensure a fair hearing.

If so, the court may order a *preliminary* hearing where it appears that it is *necessary* for a party to attend court, so as to ensure that she *understands what she must do to comply* with the special directions (CPR 27.4). The court must, however, have regard to the desirability of *limiting the expense* to the parties of attending court.

Where there is a preliminary hearing, the court will deal with as many aspects of the case as it can at that hearing. This includes considering whether to fix a date for the final hearing (if it has not done so already), and giving any other, appropriate directions (CPR 27.6(5)).

j. Directions

The court also has a general power to add to, vary, or revoke, directions (CPR 27.7).

This should be used to further the overriding objective by actively managing cases. A party may invite the court to make a particular direction (PD 27 at [2.4]). This includes requesting an order in the directions questionnaire that, *unless* a statement of case is verified by a statement of truth, within a *prescribed* period of time, it should *automatically* be struck out.

4. Pre-action protocols & Practice Direction – Pre-Action Conduct

Pre-action protocols explain the *conduct*, and set out the *steps*, that the court would *normally* expect parties to take *before* commencing proceedings (see appendix E). Fifteen pre-action protocols are currently in force. Where no specific pre-action protocol applies, however, as is the case in most claims that are allocated to the small claims track, the parties are expected to comply with the Practice Direction – Pre-Action Conduct ("the Practice Direction").

a. Objectives

The Practice Direction requires the parties to *exchange sufficient information* before commencing proceedings, so that the following six objectives are achieved.

First, to *understand* each other's position. Secondly, to *make decisions* about how to proceed. Thirdly, to *try to settle* the issues, without proceedings. Fourthly, to *consider* a form of *alternative dispute resolution* to assist with settlement. Fifthly, to support the *efficient management* of proceedings. Sixthly, to *reduce the costs* of resolving the dispute.

b. Reasonable & proportionate

Reasonable and *proportionate* steps should be taken by the parties to *identify*, *narrow*, and *resolve*, the *legal*, *factual*, or *expert*, issues. The court will *only* expect reasonable and proportionate steps. *Costs* incurred in complying with the requirements of pre-action conduct should be proportionate.

The court expects proportionate *correspondence* and *information* to be exchanged.

Proportionate steps before issuing a claim usually *include* the following.

First, the *claimant* writing to the *defendant*, setting out *concise* details of her claim. Secondly, the *defendant* responding to the *claimant*, within a *reasonable* period, typically no more than 14 days in a straightforward claim. Thirdly, the *parties* disclosing *key* documents that are *relevant* to the issues in dispute.

c. Non-compliance

The court will take into account non-compliance in *substance* with the terms of the relevant pre-action protocol, or the Practice Direction (see chapters 23(a)(i)(1) and 24(c)(i)). The court is not likely to be concerned with *minor* or *technical* infringements (CPR 44.2(5)(a)).

5. Statements of case

Statements of case set out a party's position.

They should enable the other party to know what is alleged against them. They are *formal* documents, and so, there are *formalities* that must be followed, *regardless* of whether a claim is allocated to the small claims track, or any other track. Statements of case set out the *key* law (where it is unusual), and the *material* facts, the *issues* that are in dispute, and provide *concise* particulars of what the *claim* is *about*, or on what the *defence* is *based*.

a. Types

A claim form, particulars of claim (where not in the claim form), defence, counterclaim, additional claim under Part 20, and reply to defence, all qualify as "statements of case". Upon receipt of a defence, a claimant may serve a reply to the defence.

b. Rules & practice directions

Although the *strict* rules of *evidence* do *not* apply to a claim that is allocated to the small claims track, this does *not* mean that the rules relating to *statements of case* do not apply. The rules and practice directions prescribing the requirements for statements of case are *not* disapplied (CPR 27.2(1)). It is prudent to invest time, then, to become *familiar* with these rules, so as to *comply* with them, and *identify* where the other party has failed *substantially* to comply.

To that end, the following is intended to provide an insight into relevant considerations when drafting statements of case, in the context of a claim following a road traffic collision. It is not intended to be comprehensive. There are other, excellent professional texts on drafting statements of case, with which this practical guide is not in competition, but rather, seeks to complement.

i. Legible & intelligible

When completing any court form by hand, use capital letters, and black ink. This is, of course, so that it is legible; and that, if it is scanned and photocopied, copies are also legible.

Most statements of case are typed. All the necessary elements to establish a claim or defence must be pleaded. Facts should be limited to those necessary to understand the claim or defence.

ii. Heading

A statement of case must have a heading.

This includes the name of the court in the top, left-hand corner, which should be capitalised, emboldened, and underlined. The claim number should be in the top, right-hand corner, emboldened, and underlined. Underneath the name of the court, on the left-hand side, '**BETWEEN:**' should appear. Below this, the names of the parties should be set out, capitalised, centralised, and emboldened.

The status of a party should appear in the line underneath their name, underlined, and aligned to the right-hand side of the page. 'And' is used in civil proceedings, not 'v'. The latter is the convention in criminal proceedings. Following that, between horizontal tram lines, the form of the statement of case should be stated, capitalised, centralised, and emboldened. For example: '**DEFENCE AND COUNTERCLAIM**'.

iii. Numbers & figures

Pages, paragraphs, and lists should be numbered consecutively. Numbers and dates must be expressed as figures.

iv. Authority & evidence

Statements of case *may* do any of the following (PD 16 at [13.3]).

First, refer to any point of law on which the claim or defence is based. Secondly, give the name of any witness who it is proposed to call. Thirdly, attach to, or serve with, the statement of case, a copy of any document which is considered *necessary* to the claim or defence (including any expert's report).

These are *not* mandatory, however, unless it would *help the court* to further the *overriding objective*, by ensuring that the case is dealt with *expeditiously* and *fairly*.

v. Particularity

Statements of case are of *fundamental* importance.

Often, they are too general, or too detailed. Too general, and a statement of case will fail to set out the material detail of law and fact necessary for a claim or defence to succeed. Too detailed, repetitive, and encumbered with unnecessary authority, however, and, at best, the court is likely to skim over it.

The art (of course) is in finding the appropriate balance. Allegations must be particularised. For example, after a road traffic collision, an allegation of negligence should list the ways in which a party is alleged to have been negligent. If it is claimed that the defendant was negligent in that she drove too fast for the road conditions, then, it must be set out.

vi. Contributory negligence

Where contributory negligence is alleged, often in a defence, or as an alternative in the particulars of claim following a road traffic collision, the party so alleging should set it out (PD 16 at [13.3(1)]).

There is no need to put a percentage on the alleged negligence of a party. If contributory negligence is still relied on in closing submissions, a figure can be suggested, so as to take into account the oral evidence.

vii. Endorsement

Where a legal representative has drafted a statement of case, it should bear the signature of the person who has drafted it. If drafted by a legal representative as a member or employee of a firm, it should be signed in the name of the firm (PD 5A at [2.1]).

viii. Statement of truth

Statements of case must be verified by a statement of truth (CPR 22.1(1)(a)).

1. Particulars of claim

Where particulars of claim are not included in the claim form, the form of words for the statement of truth is (PD 16 at [3.4]): '[I believe / The claimant believes] that the facts stated in these particulars of claim are true.' Where it is signed by a lay client, 'I believe' are the first words; where it is signed by a legal representative, 'The claimant believes' are the first words.

2. Who

The statement of truth must be signed by a party, her litigation friend, or the legal representative of the party, or her litigation friend (PD 22 at [3.1]). She must also print her name clearly beneath her signature (PD 22 at [3.9]). Entering a name on an online form satisfies the requirement for a statement of truth to be signed (PD 7E at [10]).

a. Legal representative

Where a party is legally represented, the legal representative may sign the statement of truth on her client's behalf. It will refer to *her client's* belief, and *not* her own. She must state the *capacity* in which she is signing, and the *name* of her firm (PD 22 at [3.7]). A legal representative signing a statement of truth must do so in her *own* name, and not that of her *firm* or *employer* (PD 22 at [3.10]).

Where a legal representative signed a statement of truth, her signature *will* be taken by the court as her *confirmation* of the following three facts (PD 22 at [3.8]).

First, her client has *authorised* her to do so. Secondly, before signing, she explained to her client that, in signing the statement of truth, she would be *confirming* her client's belief that the facts stated in the document are true. Thirdly, before signing, she informed her client of the possible *consequences* to *her client*, if subsequently it appeared that her client did not have an honest belief in the truth of those facts.

These facts are useful to have at your fingertips when *resisting* an application for relief from sanctions, when there has been a *serious* and *significant* breach, caused *solely* by the *legal representative*.

b. Companies & partnerships

For registered companies and corporations, a director, treasurer, secretary, chief executive, manager, or other officer, may sign (PD 22 at [3.5(1)]). For partnerships, a partner, person having control or management the partnership, or legal representative, may sign (PD 22 at [3.6]).

c. Insurers

An insurer may sign a statement of truth on behalf of a party, where the insurer has a financial interest in the result of proceedings, brought wholly, or partially, by, or against, that party (PD 22 at [3.6A]). Where insurers are conducting proceedings on behalf of many claimants or defendants, it may be signed by a senior person responsible for the case at a lead insurer, subject to the following three conditions (PD 22 at [3.6B]).

First, the person signing must specify the *capacity* in which she signs. Secondly, the statement of truth must be a statement that the *lead* insurer believes that the facts stated in the statement of case are true. Thirdly, the court may order a statement of truth to *also* be signed by one or more of the *parties*.

3. Default

If a party fails to verify her statement of case by a statement of truth, the *court* may strike it out. A *party* may apply for a strike out order.

A party's statement of case *remains* effective *until* it is struck out, however, that party *cannot* rely on it as *evidence* of any of the matters set out within it (CPR 22.2). Where a statement of case is not verified by a statement of truth, in practice, the court will make an *unless* order. That is, unless the statement of case is verified by a certain date, it will *automatically* be struck out (PD 22 at [4.2]).

6. Claim form

There are two different methods for commencing proceedings. In general, this depends on whether there is a *substantial dispute of fact*. This chapter provides practical guidance as to *how* to complete a claim form, and what are the *material* details, including how to work out the *issue* fee, *hearing* fee, and *fixed* costs.

a. Substantial dispute of fact

In general, where there is no substantial dispute of fact, the *alternative* method of commencing proceedings may be used. Where this "Part 8" procedure is used – so called because the relevant CPR is 8 – Form N208 is the correct claim form. Although there is nothing to stop a Part 8 claim being allocated to the small claims track, in practice, it is uncommon.

Where there is a substantial dispute of fact, generally, the "Part 7" procedure should be used. The claim form spans two pages. It is Form N1. To commence proceedings, a claim form is issued, which the court seals with its official seal. Unless there is an extension, the claim form must be served within *four* months of the date of issue on the claim form (CPR 7.5).

b. Court

On page one, in the top, right-hand corner, the name of the court should appear. If using Money Claim Online, this box will be automatically completed. Otherwise, this will be 'County Court Money Claims Centre'.

c. Parties

The name of the claimant(s) and defendant(s) should appear on the right-hand side.

i. Individuals

If they are individuals, this should include their title, and their full name. If they have recently changed their name, after their name '(formerly ...)' should follow. A protected party should include the name of her litigation friend. For example: 'Ms Sarah Smith (by Mrs Helen Smith, her litigation friend)'.

ii. Companies & partnerships

For a partnership, the name of the partnership, followed by '(a firm)' should be used. For example, 'Smith & Smith (a firm)'. For sole traders, the title and full name of the individuals, followed by 'trading as ...' should follow. For example: 'Ms Sarah Smith, trading as Smith's Bakery'.

Limited companies should include the word 'limited'. To check whether a company has limited liability, search the website of 'Companies House' (beta.companieshouse.gov.uk). The company number, registered office address, and company type (private or public limited company), are all available.

iii. Insurers

The European Communities (Rights against Insurers) Regulations 2002 (SI 2002/3061) allows claimants to bring proceedings arising out of road traffic collisions against the insurer of the defendant vehicle. This does *not* extinguish the right of the claimant to bring an action against the defendant.

d. Address

The postal address and postcode of the claimant(s) and defendant(s) should be provided.

i. Individuals

For individuals, this is the *residential* address. *Even* with legal representation, so that the legal representative's address is used, a *residential* or *business* address must also be provided.

ii. Businesses

For businesses, the *business* address can be used. The *registered office* of a limited company must be used. Companies House can be used to identify the registered office address of a (public or private) limited company.

e. Detail

Concise details of the claim should be pleaded.

For example: 'The claimant claims damages and other losses arising from a road traffic collision on 24 October 2019, caused by the negligent driving of the defendant.' A claim that is allocated to the small claims track is *un*likely to include any issues under the Human Rights Act 1998.

Particulars of claim can be pleaded on page two of the claim form, but usually, they are *attached* as a *separate* document. If so, the words 'to follow' should be crossed out.

f. Value

Underneath the heading 'Value', a typical sentence might read: 'Damages not exceeding £10,000.' The amount claimed (the amount in dispute, including interest) should be pleaded in the bottom, right-hand corner of the first page.

g. Interest

Any claim for interest must be particularised (CPR 16.4(2)).

Failure to do so will enable a defendant to point to *breach* of the rules of court, lack of *notice* that there is a claim for interest, and consequent *unfairness*, which all weigh in favour of disallowing any award of interest.

h. Preferred hearing centre

The claimant must state the *preferred* county court hearing centre.

i. Individual

Where the *defendant* is an *individual*, and the claim has *not* been sent to a county court hearing centre, the claim will be sent to the *defendant's* home court in two circumstances (PD 7E at [12.1]). First, if the defendant applies to *set aside* or *vary* judgment. Secondly, if *either* party makes an application, which can*not* be dealt with without a hearing.

ii. Not an individual

Where the defendant is *not* an individual, and *either* of the above circumstances apply, the claim will be sent to the county court hearing centre which serves the *claimant's* address for service. This should be stated on the claim form (PD 7E at [12.2]).

iii. Transfer

If a defence is filed to all or part of the claim, and the parties have filed directions questionnaires, the proceedings will be *transferred* as follows (PD 7E at [12.3]).

Where the defendant is an *individual*, and the claim is for a *specified* amount of money, the claim will be transferred to the *defendant's* home court. If a *different* preferred court is *specified* by the claimant or defendant in the respective *directions questionnaires*, the claim will be transferred to *that* court. In the event of a conflict, the judge will decide. Otherwise, the claim will be transferred to the *claimant's* preferred court.

i. Address for service

The address for service of both parties must be provided.

i. Claimant

Where a claimant is represented, the address for service is that of the legal representative. This must be in the UK. This includes the postal address and postcode. DX, fax, and email *may* be given.

Where an *individual* has conduct of a case for a *company that is not represented*, the *business* address of *that person* should be used (as opposed to the *registered office* address). This is so that correspondence is *actually* received.

ii. Defendant

The address for service of a *defendant* is where the defendant is *(last) known to live* or *carry on business*. The defendant can provide an address for service, such as the name of her legal representative. Where the defendant is *not* represented, and the defendant has *not* otherwise stated her address for service, CPR 6.9 prescribes the rules for service.

j. Fees & costs

The issue fee, hearing fee, and legal representative's costs should all be provided in the bottom, right-hand corner of the first page (see chapter 23(b) and (c)).

k. Remission

A claimant can apply for help with fees for a court hearing. This is called "fee remission". Form EX160A provides detailed guidance. In summary, only *individuals* can apply.

For eligibility, a claimant must satisfy one of the following criteria.

First, no savings, investments, or only a small amount of the same, and in receipt of certain benefits. Secondly, on a low income. If successful, there may not be *any* fee, or, if there is, there may be money off that fee.

l. Issue

If using the County Court Money Claims Centre ("the CCMC"), the postal address is PO Box 527, Salford M5 0BY. Copies of the completed claim form – one for the court, and one for each defendant – together with the issue fee, should be posted to the CCMC. A copy of the claim form should be retained, so that the claimant has a copy. It is advisable that the fee is paid by cheque to 'HM Courts & Tribunals Service'.

The court will then "issue" the claim. Although the claimant can elect to "serve" proceedings herself, it is advisable to follow the general rule, so that the court serves each defendant by first class post. As the centre is not open to the public visiting in person, it can be contacted by telephone on 0300 123 1372, or email using ccmccustomerenquiries@hmcts.gsi.gov.uk.

7. Particulars of claim

Not all statements of case are equal.

If a *defence* is struck out, in principle, the claim *may* still fail. If the *particulars of claim* are struck out, however, the claim *cannot* succeed. The burden is on the party bringing the claim.

a. Within claim form or separate document

Particulars of claim may be included *in* the claim form or a *separate* document. There is limited space, both in the paper, *and* the online claim form. Where the particulars of claim are in a separate document, that document *may* be served with the claim form, but *must* be served within 14 days of the claim form (CPR 7.4(1)).

Particulars of claim that are served separately to the claim form must also contain four details (PD 16 at [3.8]).

First, the name of the court in which the case is proceeding. Secondly, the claim number. Thirdly, the title of proceedings. Fourthly, the claimant's address for service. If not included within the claim form, or served separately, the claim form must state that the particulars of claim will follow (CPR 16.2(2)).

b. Contents

Particulars of claim must contain three details (CPR 16.4).

First, a *concise* statement of the facts on which the claimant relies. Secondly, details of any *interest* that is sought (see below). Thirdly, 'other matters' that are set out in a practice direction. Those relevant to claims that are allocated to the small claims track, include personal injury (PD 16 at [4]), where a claim for general damages as a result of pain, suffering, and loss of amenity, is not more than £1,000.

c. Breach of contract

There are specific points which must be set out in claims alleging *breach of contract*.

i. Written

In a claim based upon a *written* agreement, there are three requirements (PD 16 at [7.3]).

First, a copy of the *contract* or documents constituting the *agreement* should be *attached* to, or *served* with, the particulars of claim. Secondly, the *original* should be available at the hearing. Thirdly, any *general conditions of sale* incorporated into the contract should be attached (where bulky, the relevant parts suffice).

ii. Oral

In a claim based upon an *oral* agreement, there are five requirements (PD 16 at [7.4]).

First, the contractual *words* used. Secondly, *by* whom. Thirdly, *to* whom. Fourthly, *when*. Fifthly, *where* they were spoken.

iii. Conduct

In a claim based upon an agreement by *conduct*, there are four requirements (PD 16 at [7.5]).

First, the *conduct* relied on. Secondly, *by* whom. Thirdly, *when*. Fourthly, *where* the acts constituting the conduct were done.

d. Personal injury

Where general damages following personal injury for £1,000 or less are claimed, there are four points that must be set out (PD 16 at [4]).

First, the claimant's *date of birth*. Secondly, brief details of the *injuries* suffered. Thirdly, a *schedule* of details of past and future expenses and losses claimed must be attached to, or contained within, the particulars of claim. Fourthly, where the evidence of a medical practitioner is relied on, the claimant must attach to, or serve with, her particulars of claim, a *report from that practitioner* about the injuries which are alleged.

e. Statement of facts

In principle, in a claim following a road traffic collision, where there is no counterclaim, the *defendant* does *not* have to prove that the *mechanism* of the collision, or even that the *location* of the collision, is that which is set out in the defence. The claim may still fail.

The burden is on the *claimant* to persuade the court that, on a balance of probabilities, the collision occurred as pleaded in the *particulars of claim*.

If a *defendant* can show that the *mechanism* of the collision, or even that the *location* of the collision, is *inconsistent* with the *particulars of claim*, then, the court should *dismiss* the claim.

Accordingly, particulars of claim can be particularly helpful to *defendants*. Especially if the *claimant's* evidence is *inconsistent* with what is pleaded in her *particulars of claim*. Where this is the case, this should form the basis of closing submissions (see chapter 21(b)(iii)(2)).

f. Considerations following a road traffic collision

There are many claims allocated to the small claims track following a road traffic collision. Accordingly, *potentially* relevant considerations when drafting particulars of claim in such an action are suggested below. Not *every* consideration will be relevant to *every* claim; *different* considerations will be relevant to *different* claims.

Particulars of claim should set out a *concise* statement of the facts *on which the claimant relies*. Written evidence can flesh out the meat of the facts. Only the *material*, factual bones on which the claim relies *must* be set out. The test, then – so as to filter out facts that do *not* need to be set out in the particulars of claim – is whether the fact is *necessary* for the claim to *succeed*.

i. When, where & who

What was the date, time, and location of the accident? Who (or what company) is responsible for each vehicle? Is the claim subrogated (that is, does an insurance company have a right to pursue a third party that caused an insurance loss to the insured)?

ii. Road layout

What was the name of the road, junction or island? How many lanes were there? Were there traffic lights? Signage? Road markings? If so, were the lanes on the roundabout clearly separated by broken white lines?

iii. Traffic

Light traffic? Or gridlocked? What were the type of vehicles on the road: personal cars only, heavy goods vehicles, or slow-moving tractors and farm machinery?

iv. Weather

What were the weather conditions? Light or dark? Was there any street lighting? If so, was it on? Was it snowing, hailing, or raining? Was the road wet? What was the visibility?

v. Vehicles

What were the makes, models, and vehicle registrations of the relevant vehicles? What direction(s) were these vehicles traveling? Southeast, towards Reading, or in different directions (and, if so, which direction were the relevant vehicles travelling)?

vi. Speed

What was the speed limit? How fast were the relevant vehicles travelling? Were these speeds *appropriate* for the *traffic* and *weather* conditions? Was the claimant's vehicle stationary at the time of the collision? If so, was the engine off, and the handbrake on? If it was a manual transmission, was the gear stick in neutral?

vii. Proximity

Where were the relevant vehicles in relation to each other? Was the claimant's vehicle in front of, level with, or behind, the defendant's vehicle? How many metres behind the claimant's vehicle was the defendant's vehicle? If there were multiple lanes on approach to a junction, was the claimant in the left-hand, or the right-hand lane? Which lane was the defendant in?

viii. Perception

When did the claimant first see the defendant's vehicle before the collision (if at all)? When did the defendant first see the claimant's vehicle? Was a visual (hand) or audible (horn) signal used to notify the defendant of the claimant's vehicle?

ix. Objective intention

What were the parties' objective intentions? Were both vehicles indicating right? Was the claimant's vehicle positioned to the left of the lane, broadcasting an intention to turn left, or in the centre of the lane, projecting an intention to go straight on?

What (if any) mirrors were checked before changing speed, or direction? Was the left blind spot checked before turning left, so as to check for cyclists?

x. Subjective intention

To where was the claimant intending on travelling? Was it to work? If so, was it a routine journey, so that the claimant was familiar with the road layout and traffic conditions for that time of day?

xi. Mechanism

What was the mechanism of collision? Was the claimant's vehicle hit by the defendant's vehicle, when the latter was emerging from a side road? Or was it a rear-end shunt? Was the claimant's vehicle hit whilst parked? Was the collision in a car park, on a roundabout, or involving vehicles changing lanes? Or was it a concertina collision? Did the defendant swerve into the claimant's lane?

xii. Mitigation

Was there time to take defensive action, so as to avoid collision? Was it possible for the claimant to steer, brake, or sound the horn, so as to avoid the defendant's vehicle entirely, or at least warn the defendant of the claimant's presence? If not, why?

xiii. Damage

Where was the damage to the relevant vehicles? Modest scratch, moderate dent, or heavy impact, to the tailgate of the claimant's vehicle, causing the bonnet of the defendant's vehicle to crumple severely? Is there an engineers' report, commenting upon the damage to one of the vehicles?

Is there an estimate for repair? Or just an invoice for the repairs? If so, does it particularise the repairs that were in fact undertaken?

g. Interest

Where interest is sought, the following *must* be pleaded (CPR 16.4(2)).

First, whether it is under the terms of a *contract*, another enactment (and, if so, *which*), or on some other basis (and, if so, *what* that basis is).

Secondly, if the claim is for a specified amount of money: 1) the percentage rate at which interest is claimed; 2) the date from which it is claimed; 3) the date to which it is calculated (which must be no later than the date on which the claim form is issued); 4) the total amount of interest claimed to the date of calculation; and 5) after that date, the daily rate at which interest accrues.

i. Contractual

If a term for interest has been *agreed* between the parties, it should be pleaded.

In *Chaplair Ltd v Kumari* [2015] EWCA Civ 798, [2015] HLR 39, the Court of Appeal held that a county court judge could make an award of costs in favour of a landlord in a claim for rent arrears allocated to the small claims track. The terms of the *lease* allowed recovery of the *costs* of legal proceedings.

Where a party has a *contractual right* to costs, it is *not* restricted to fixed costs. That is, provided that there has been no conduct on behalf of that party, so as to disentitle the same to the exercise by the court of its discretion, in accordance with that contractual entitlement. The same *principle* applies to a contractual entitlement to *interest*.

ii. Statutory

There are two relevant statutory provisions in relation to interest for claims that are allocated to the small claims track. If you can rely on a contractually agreed rate of interest, do so, as it is likely to be greater than that awarded by the court. That is, unless you have a business-to-business contract, in which you can imply a term for interest.

1. County Courts Act 1984

The decision *whether* to award interest under section 69 of the County Courts Act 1984 is *discretionary*. It reflects the fact that a claimant has been denied use of a sum that the court has found due. The *rate* and *period* that interest accrues is also discretionary. The yearly rate of eight percent is often claimed, however, in practice, two-to-four percent is awarded.

2. Late Payment of Commercial Debts (Interest) Act 1998

The Late Payment of Commercial Debts (Interest) Act 1998 adds implied terms in business-to-business contracts. It prescribes that a claimant will be awarded three benefits.

First, *at least* eight percent interest a year on the price of goods or services. Secondly, a *fixed sum*. Thirdly, *reasonable costs of recovering* the debt.

The implied term is for *simple* interest, at a *fixed* rate, set twice a year by adding eight percent to the Bank of England's official Base Rate. The rate that was current when interest began to run is that which should be claimed. The date that interest starts to run depends on when the contract was made. Interest ceases on payment of the principal sum.

For a debt below £1,000, the fixed sum is £40. For a debt of at least £1,000, but less than £10,000, the fixed sum is £70. For a debt of £10,000 or more, the fixed sum is £100.

Reasonable costs of recovering a debt are likely to include instructing a legal representative, and pre-action costs.

iii. Personal injury

Where general damages are awarded in claims following personal injury, interest is awarded at two percent from the date of service of the claim form (*Birkett v Hayes* [1982] 1 WLR 816).

8. Defence (& counterclaim)

To defend against a claim, a defence *must* be filed (CPR 15.2) and served (CPR 15.6). The time limit is within 14 days of service of the particulars of claim; or 28 days if the defendant has acknowledged service.

a. Response

A defence ought to respond to each allegation in the particulars of claim. There are three responses (CPR 16.5).

First, denied. Secondly, unable to admit or deny, but which the claimant is required to prove. Thirdly, admitted.

Where an allegation is denied, the reasons for doing so must be stated.

If a defendant has a different version of events to that set out in the particulars of claim, the defendant's version must be stated. Where a *specific* allegation has not been dealt with, but the *nature of the defence in relation to that allegation* has been set out, the court will require the claimant to prove the allegation.

The court will take *any* allegation relating to an amount of *money* that is claimed to be *proved*, unless it is expressly admitted. Subject to the above, the court will take *any* allegation that is *not* dealt with in a defence to be *admitted* (CPR 16.5(4) and (5)).

Admitted facts do *not* need to be proved. Authority and evidence supporting them, therefore, is irrelevant; the court will not consider them.

b. Address for service

If two conditions are satisfied, the defendant must provide an address for service in the defence (PD 16 at [10.4]).

First, the *defendant* is an *individual*. Secondly, the *claim form* does *not* contain an address at which she *resides*, carries on *business*, or contains an *incorrect* address.

Where the defendant's address for service is not where she resides, or carries on business, she must still provide the address, including the postcode (PD 16 at [10.5]).

c. Individuals

Where a *defendant* to a *claim*, or *claimant* to a *counterclaim* is an *individual*, she must provide her *date of birth* (if known) in the acknowledgment of service, admission, defence, defence and counterclaim, reply, or other response (PD 16 at [10.7]).

d. Counterclaim

A counterclaim is a separate claim.

Accordingly, the rules and practice directions for particulars of claim apply (see chapter 7). Where there is a defence to the claimant's claim, and a counterclaim against the claimant, the statement of case is known as a 'defence and counterclaim'. The counterclaim should follow the defence, so that, if the facts set out in the defence are relied on in the counterclaim (which is usually the case), this can be succinctly stated in a single sentence.

Where a counterclaim is filed with the defence, permission is not required (CPR 20.4(2)(a)). Issuing a counterclaim will attract an issue fee, however, based on the amount claimed in the counterclaim (see chapter 23(b)(i)). To defend against a counterclaim, the claimant must file and serve a defence to the counterclaim (CPRs 15.2, 15.6 and 20.2).

9. Reply to the defence (& counterclaim)

The key points are that: a *reply to a defence* is *optional*; and a *defence* to a *counterclaim* is *mandatory*. Where a counterclaim is not defended, the defendant may request that default judgment is entered on the counterclaim.

a. Reply

A reply to a defence may be filed and served with the claimant's directions questionnaire (CPR 15.8). The deadline is no less than 14 days after service of the provisional allocation notice (CPR 26.3(6)(b)(i)). This is form N149A.

b. Defence

A claimant *must* serve a defence to a counterclaim. The rules and practice directions relating to defences apply (see chapter 8). Where there is a reply to a defence, and a defence to a counterclaim, the statement of case is known as a "reply to the defence and counterclaim".

A party's statements of case must not be incompatible (for example, that the claimant's particulars of claim are incompatible with her reply to the defence). To the extent that they are, they risk being struck out.

10. Directions questionnaires

The *court* must further the overriding objective by actively managing cases: where appropriate, encouraging parties to use alternative dispute resolution; fixing timetables, or otherwise controlling the progress of the case; and giving directions to ensure that the final hearing proceeds both quickly, and efficiently (CPR 1.4(2)). The *parties* are under a duty to help the court to do so, which is one reason why *directions questionnaires* are important.

a. Notice of proposed allocation

If a defendant files a defence, a court officer will do two things (CPR 26.3(1)(a)).

First, provisionally decide the track which appears to be most suitable for the claim. Secondly, serve on each party a notice of proposed allocation. This is Form N194A.

The notice of proposed allocation will do four things (CPR 26.3(1)(b)).

First, *specify any matter to be complied with* by the date prescribed in the notice. Secondly, *require the parties to file* a completed directions questionnaire, and *serve copies* on all other parties. Thirdly, state the *address of the court office* to which the directions questionnaire must be returned. Fourthly, inform the parties *how* to obtain the directions questionnaire.

b. Filing

The directions questionnaire for the small claims track is form N180. The court will *always* serve the appropriate directions questionnaire on an *un*represented party (CPR 26.3(1B)).

The questionnaire should be returned by the date provided for in the notice of allocation. It can*not* be extended by the agreement of the parties (CPR 26.3(6A)). The name of the court to which the questionnaire must be *returned* may be *different* from that in which the claim was *issued*. If so, ensure that the questionnaire is returned to the *correct* court.

c. Default

If a party fails to comply with the notice of proposed allocation by the specified date, the court will serve a *further* notice on that party, requiring them to comply within *seven* days. If the party *still* fails to comply, that party's statement of case will be struck out, *without* further order of the court (CPR 26.3(7A)).

If a *claimant* fails to file a directions questionnaire, the court may *strike out* the claim; where the *defendant* is in default, *judgment may be entered* against her (PD 26 at [2.5(3)]).

A party who was in default will *not* normally be entitled to an order for the *costs* of any application to *set aside* or *vary* that order, *nor* the costs of attending a case management conference. *Unless* the court considers that it is *unjust*, that party *will* be ordered to pay the costs that the default caused to any *other* party (CPR 26.3(10)).

d. Informing the court

If the claim has been settled, or if the claim is settled in the future, so that there is no need for a hearing, *the parties* must let the court know *immediately*. *Both* parties are under the same duty to help the *court* to allocate an *appropriate* share of the court's resources to the case, while taking into account the need to allot resources to *other* cases.

Every effort should be made to settle. *Both* parties are under a duty to consider whether the dispute can be settled *without* a hearing. This can be achieved by a direct discussion between the parties, negotiation between the legal representatives of the parties, or mediation.

e. Small Claims Mediation Service

Mediation is a *confidential* process, giving the *parties* control over any agreement. Settlement may be *facilitated,* but it cannot be *imposed*. Although a mediator *may* be able to assist with what the law says in a particular circumstance, she will do so from a *neutral* perspective, *dispassionately*, and with *no* interest in any agreement.

Offers can be made, without influencing what happens if the claim is resolved after a court hearing. This can enable the parties to try to reach an agreement, *without* compromising their positions, should the claim go to a final hearing. Positions are reserved in absence of agreement.

If an *agreement* is reached, reduced to writing, and signed, it is *binding* like any other *contract*. The terms of any agreement can be inserted into a "Tomlin order", so that they can be *enforced* by the court, should there be a breach. As a mediated settlement is *voluntary*, however, freely agreed terms of settlement are usually honoured, *without* the need to enforce them.

In light of the above, the *free*, and *confidential*, Small Claims Mediation Service is deserving of serious consideration. It is *convenient*, as it is usually carried out over the *telephone* in under an hour, at a time that is suitable for both parties. It is also *quicker* than waiting for a court hearing. It is *voluntary*, in that the parties are not obliged to settle; the claim may progress to a final hearing, should agreement not be possible.

The *parties* have to *agree* before the case may be referred to the Small Claims Mediation Service, however, which is why section A1 of the directions questionnaire is so important. This section enquires whether a party agrees to the claim being so referred. If all parties agree to mediation, their contact details will be passed to the Small Claims Mediation Service, who will contact them, and arrange a mutually convenient appointment.

Contact will be made within normal working hours, that is, Monday to Friday, from 09:00 to 17:00, excluding bank holidays. Of course, having agreed to mediation, the parties should engage proactively, and in good faith.

f. Stay

Upon the request of the parties, the court will "stay" proceedings for one month, and the court will notify the parties of the same (CPR 26.4(2)).

The court can extend the stay until such *date*, or for such specified *period*, as the court considers appropriate (CPR 26.4(3)). The *claimant* must inform the court if a settlement is reached (CPR 26.4(4)). Otherwise, if the end of the period of the stay has been reached, the court will give such *directions* as to the *management* of the case as the court considers *appropriate* (CPR 26.4(5)).

g. Track

The directions questionnaire asks the parties whether the small claims track is the appropriate track. This is the opportunity to give reasons why it is not, if that is the case.

h. Hearing centre

The county court hearing centre closest to the party that is completing the questionnaire is likely to be the preferred venue for hearing the claim. If a party, for example, has a registered disability, childcare commitments, or is a carer for another, vulnerable adult, these are good reasons justifying the claim being heard in the county court hearing centre that is nearest to that party.

If a *claimant* files a request for judgment in the county court, which includes an amount of money *to be decided* by the court, in accordance with the procedure for obtaining default judgment, the claim will be sent to the *preferred* hearing centre (CPR 12.5A(1)).

CPR 26 provides the circumstances in which defended cases may be sent from one county court hearing centre, or court office, to another (CPR 26.1(1)(a1)). CPR 26.2A prescribes the circumstances in which money claims may be transferred *within* the county court.

i. Experts

In claims following a road traffic collision, for example, there are an increasing number of claimants pleading that, *although* their vehicle has been *repaired*, nevertheless, there remains *diminution* in the *market* value of their vehicle.

The evidence relied on is often in the form of a (main) report, or a number of (subsidiary) reports that are appendixed to the main report, in which an opinion is expressed that there is diminution in value. Frequently, there is a statement that is not dissimilar to that which it is common to see in expert reports. That is, that the person who is offering her opinion is aware of her duty to the court (as opposed to the party that has instructed her to write the report).

If so, the importance of section D2 of the directions questionnaire is *vital*.

It is second only to the court's directions for the hearing. If there was *no request* to rely on expert evidence by a party in her directions questionnaire, and the court has *not given permission*, there is a robust argument that expert evidence *cannot* be relied upon. Otherwise, there would be a breach of the overriding objective to enforce compliance with rules, practice directions, and court orders.

To this end, it is also important to check whether a party has filed and served any proposed directions in a *separate* document. Again, if there is no indication that permission to rely upon expert evidence is sought, then, it can be persuasively argued that a party has failed to help the court to achieve the overriding objective.

An appropriate share of the court's resources will not have been allotted to the claim because, the court having given the parties a *time estimate* for the final hearing, an *application* will now have to be made at the *outset* of the hearing for permission to rely on expert evidence, thereby *increasing* this time estimate. Also, the parties can be argued to have been placed on an unequal footing, as the party resisting the application for permission has proceeded on the basis that permission has not been granted.

j. Witnesses

It is important to state *how many* witnesses will attend the hearing, so that the court can determine whether the hearing will last more than a day. With this information, the court is able to provide an *accurate* time estimate of the hearing. When an expert, or a witness, will be unavailable over the following six months, due to holiday, or professional commitments, this should be set out.

k. Interpreters

If a party or a witness requires an interpreter, the relevant box should be *ticked*, together with the *type* of interpreter required. If the matter proceeds to a *final* hearing, the witness *cannot* sufficiently understand

English, there is only one witness statement in *English*, and there is *no* interpreter, the court is *much* more likely to strike out that witness' evidence if the box for an interpreter is not ticked 'yes'.

In some circumstances, the *court* will *arrange* and meet the *cost* of an interpreter. In general, however, civil cases that do *not* involve possession of property, or committal, do *not* qualify for legal aid. In any event, three conditions must be satisfied.

First, inability to pay for an interpreter. Secondly, ineligibility for legal aid. Thirdly, lack of a friend or family member who can act as an interpreter. Those who can only follow proceedings with a Welsh interpreter, however, *are* entitled to one.

If a party *subsequently* becomes aware of the need for an interpreter, the court, and the other party should be notified *immediately*. This is likely substantially to affect the time estimate of the final hearing, and there is likely to be a direction ordering the parties to notify the court immediately where this is the case.

Failure to act promptly may result in that witness not being able to give evidence, and costs consequences, on the basis that a party has behaved unreasonably.

l. Signature

The directions questionnaire must be signed by the party, legal representative, or litigation friend.

m. Further information

The court may order a party to provide *further* information on the court's own initiative (CPR 27.2(3)). In practice, this power is typically used where a *statement of case* is *unclear*. The court may go further, and strike it out, where: a statement of case is *so* incoherent that it makes no sense; or, if there *is* a coherent set of facts, *even* where those facts are true, they do not disclose any legally recognisable claim or defence (PD 3A at [1.4]).

The court will necessarily be *circumspect*, however, before deciding to exercise this *draconian* power, and thereby *extinguish* a claim or defence.

n. Other directions

A *party* may invite the court to make a *particular* direction (PD 27 at [2.4]). The best place to do so is in the directions questionnaire. The court also has a general power to add to, vary, or revoke, directions (CPR 27.7).

11. Allocation

In general, a claim will be allocated to a track when all parties have filed their directions questionnaires (CPR 26.5(1)(a)). This means that, before a claim is allocated, the court will have the benefit of the statements of case, and the completed directions questionnaires. Once allocated, the case will be stayed for settlement discussions, mediation, or the court will give directions for the final hearing.

a. Generally suitable

There are four types of case that are 'generally suitable for the small claims track' (PD 26 at [8.1(1)(c)]).

First, consumer disputes. Secondly, accident claims. Thirdly, disputes about the ownership of goods. Fourthly, most landlord and tenant disputes, other than opposed claims under CPR 56, disputed claims for possession under CPR 55, and demotion claims.

A case involving a *disputed* allegation of *dishonesty* will usually not be suitable (PD 26 at [8.1(1)(d)]).

b. Relevant matters

The small claims track is the "normal" track for any claim which has a value of not more than £10,000 (CPR 26.6(1)). In considering whether to allocate a claim to the normal track, the court 'will also have regard to' (CPR 26.7(1)) the following nine matters (CPR 26.8(1)).

First, financial *value* (if any) of the claim. Secondly, nature of the *remedy* sought. Thirdly, likely *complexity* of the facts, law, or evidence. Fourthly, *number* of (likely) *parties*. Fifthly, value of any *counterclaim*, or other Part 20 claim, and the complexity of any matters relating to it.

Sixthly, amount of *oral evidence* which may be required. Seventhly, *importance* of the claim to persons who are *not* parties to the proceedings. Eighthly, *views* expressed by the parties. Ninthly, *circumstances* of the parties.

This list is *not* exhaustive. *Neither* is it hierarchical. Other matters that further the overriding objective *are* relevant.

i. Financial value

It is for the *court* to assess the *financial value* of a claim. In doing so, the court will disregard the following four considerations (CPR 26.8(2)).

First, any amount *not* in dispute. Secondly, any claim for *interest*. Thirdly, *costs*. Fourthly, allegations of *contributory* negligence.

1. Amount in dispute

When determining the "amount in dispute", the court will consider the following four circumstances as indicative of an amount that is *not* in dispute (PD 26 at [7.4]).

First, an amount in respect of which the defendant *admits* liability. Secondly, a sum in respect of an item forming part of a claim for which *judgment has been entered*. Thirdly, any specific sum claimed as a *distinct* item, and which the defendant *admits* that she is liable to pay. Fourthly, a sum *offered* by the *defendant*, which has been *accepted* by the *claimant* in satisfaction of any item which forms a *distinct* part of the claim.

A claim with a financial value of more than £10,000 *may* still be allocated to the small claims track (PD 26 at [8.1(2)]).

2. Admissions

Before allocation, if the defendant makes an admission that reduces the amount in dispute to a figure not more than £10,000, the normal track is the small claims track (PD 26 at [7.4(4)]).

The leading case on admissions is *Pervez Akhtar v Jordan Boland* [2014] EWCA Civ 872, [2015] 1 All ER 644.

Where an allegation made by one party ("A") is *admitted* by the other party ("B") in *un*qualified terms, A must *not* adduce evidence, or raise arguments to the effect that, that admission is not binding. The court has *no* jurisdiction to investigate a fact that has been admitted. Where judgment has been entered, for all or part of a claim, a party can*not* adduce evidence, or raise arguments, that would lead to findings *in*consistent with that judgment.

In a claim for £12,000, for example, if the defendant unequivocally admits that the claimant is entitled to judgment of £5,000, then, the only *amount in dispute* is the *balance* of the claim. That is: £7,000. Accordingly, a judge *may* allocate this claim to the small claims track. This is because the amount in dispute is less than £10,000. The court should *dis*regard any amount *not* in dispute when quantifying the financial value of a claim (CPR 26.8(2)(a)).

The court may strike out an incoherent defence.

Where a *defendant's* admission is merely *equivocal*, or *in*consistent with other allegations, the *claimant* should seek further *clarification*. If *she* fails to do so, and the *court* considers that the issues to be determined at the final hearing are uncertain, the *court* should make an order for clarification on the court's own motion. Clarification should be in *writing*.

3. Zero

A claim that has *no* financial value will be allocated to the track that is most suitable, having regard to the factors below (CPR 26.7(2)).

ii. Remedy

A claim for personal injuries where the value of the claim is not more than £10,000, but the value of the claim for damages for personal injuries is more than £1,000, for example, should not be allocated to the small claims track (CPR 26.6(1)(a)(ii)). The *nature* of the *remedy* sought in this claim means that it is *in*appropriate to allocate it to the small claims track.

The court may grant *any* final remedy that the court could grant if the claim were allocated to the *fast* track, or the *multi*-track (CPR 27.3). The court has jurisdiction to grant: an injunction; declaration; damages and interest of any amount; possession; restitution; and specific performance.

iii. Factual, legal or evidential complexity

Where the facts, law, or evidence, are *complex*, the *fast* track may be the *appropriate* track, as long as, for example: the final hearing is likely to last no longer than one day; oral evidence is limited to one expert per party in relation to any expert field; and expert evidence is limited to two fields (CPR 26.6(5)).

iv. Counterclaim / Part 20 claim

The value of a claim and any *counter*claim will *not* be added together for the purposes of allocation. If the value of the *counter*claim is larger than that of the *claim*, the court will regard the *counter*claim as determining the financial value (PD 26 at [7.7]).

v. Oral evidence

The court will not normally allocate a claim to the small claims track if it is likely to take *more* than a day (PD 26 at [8.1(2)]).

vi. Party view

This is 'an important factor', however, the *view* of the *parties* does *not* bind the court (PD 26 at [7.5]). Even if it is *not* the *normal* track, the parties may *still* elect for their dispute to be allocated to the small claims track. This may be, for example, to take advantage of modest, fixed costs, and an exception to the requirement to file pre-trial checklists.

c. Pre-allocation hearing

Where a hearing takes place *before* allocation, for example, on an application for summary judgment, the court may treat *that* hearing as an *allocation* hearing (PD 26 at [2.4(1)]).

Otherwise, an allocation hearing will only be held on the court's own initiative if it considers that it is *necessary* (PD 26 at [6.1]). If so, parties will have at least seven days' notice of the hearing in Form N153. It will give a brief explanation of the decision to order an allocation hearing (PD 26 at [6.2]).

Failure of a party to attend ("A") may lead to an *order* that *A* pay the costs of the *other* party ("B"), who did attend. Failure to pay *these* costs within the time limit may lead to the A's statement of case being struck out (PD 26 at [6.6]).

d. Challenging

If a party is dissatisfied with an order allocating the claim to a track, she may appeal, or apply to the court for the claim to be re-allocated (PD 26 at [11.1(1)]).

If the order was made *at* a hearing, at which she was *present*, *represented*, or gave *notice* that she would not attend, she should *appeal*. In any *other* case, she should *apply* to re-allocate the claim. Where there has been a change of circumstances since the claim was allocated, the court may re-allocate, on *application*, or on the court's *own* initiative (PD 26 at [11.2]).

e. Standard directions

If the case is *not* stayed, *unless* the judge specifies any other directions, *standard* directions will be given (PD 27 at Appendix B):

> 1. Each party must deliver to every other party and to the court office copies of all documents on which he intends to rely at the hearing no later than [..........] [14 days before the hearing]. (These should include the letter making the claim and the reply.)
>
> 2. The original documents must be brought to the hearing.
>
> 3. [Notice of hearing date and time allowed.]
>
> 4. The parties are encouraged to contact each other with a view to trying to settle the case or narrow the issues. However the court must be informed immediately if the case is settled by agreement before the hearing date.
>
> 5. No party may rely at the hearing on any report from an expert unless express permission has been granted by the court beforehand. Anyone wishing to rely on an expert must write to the court immediately on receipt of this Order and seek permission, giving an explanation why the assistance of an expert is necessary.
>
> NOTE: Failure to comply with the directions may result in the case being adjourned and in the party at fault having to pay costs. The parties are encouraged always to try to settle the case by negotiating with each other. The court must be informed immediately if the case is settled before the hearing.

f. Witness statements

The court must have regard to five circumstances when deciding whether to make an order for the exchange of witness statements (PD 27 at [2.5]).

First, whether *either*, or *both*, parties are *represented*. Secondly, the *amount* in dispute. Thirdly, the *nature* of the matters in dispute. Fourthly, whether the need for any party to *clarify* her case can better be dealt with by an order requiring her to give *further information*. Fifthly, the need for the parties to have access to justice, *without* undue *formality*, *cost*, or *delay*.

CPR 32 – prescribing the rules of *evidence* – does *not* apply to cases allocated to the small claims track (CPR 27.2(c)). This includes the rules prescribing *service*, *form*, and *consequences of failure to serve* witness statements.

The rule enabling the court to direct a witness statement that has not been verified by a statement of truth shall not be admissible as evidence (CPR 22.3), however, is *not* expressly disapplied.

g. Experts

No expert may give evidence at a hearing, whether written or oral, without the *permission* of the court (CPR 27.5). The *court* is under a *duty* to *restrict* expert evidence to that which is *reasonably required* to resolve the proceedings (CPR 35.1). Where required, in practice, the court usually directs that evidence is to be given by a *single joint* expert (CPR 35.7).

The form and content of expert evidence is *not* prescribed by CPR 35 – which is the rule relating to experts – with two exceptions (CPR 27.2(1)(e)).

First, experts' *overriding* duty is to the *court* (CPR 35.3). Secondly, the rules relating to *instructions* to a single joint expert (CPR 35.8).

The amount which a party may be ordered to pay for experts' fees is a sum not exceeding £750 for *each* expert (PD 27 at [7.3(2)]).

h. Special directions

Where *standard* directions are *in*sufficient, *bespoke* directions may be given (CPR 27.4(3)(b)). Particular assistance can be gleaned from the information and documentation usually required for certain types of claim (PD 27 at Appendix A and chapter 12(d)). In practice, however, the following *special* directions are used (PD 27 at Appendix C):

> The .... must clarify his case.
>
> He must do this by delivering to the court office and to the .... no later than ....
>
> [a list of ....]
>
> [details of ....]
>
> The .... must allow the .... to inspect by appointment within ... days of receiving a request to do so.
>
> The hearing will not take place at the court but at ....
>
> The .... must bring to court at the hearing the ....
>
> Signed statements setting out the evidence of all witnesses on whom each party intends to rely must be prepared and copies included in the documents mentioned in paragraph 1. This includes the evidence of the parties themselves and of any other

witness, whether or not he is going to come to court to give evidence.

The court may decide not to take into account a document [or video] or the evidence of a witness if these directions have not been complied with.

If he does not [do so] […] his [Claim] [Defence] [and Counter-claim] will be struck out and (specify consequence).

It appears to the court that expert evidence is necessary on the issue of ……….and that that evidence should be given by a single expert to be instructed by the parties jointly.

If the parties cannot agree about who to choose and what arrangements to make about paying his fee, either party MUST apply to the court for further directions. The evidence is to be given in the form of a written report. Either party may ask the expert questions and must then send copies of the questions and replies to the other party and to the court. Oral expert evidence may be allowed in exceptional circumstances but only after a further order of the court. Attention is drawn to the limit of £200 on expert's fees that may be recovered.

If either party intends to show a video as evidence he must—

> (a) contact the court at once to make arrangements for him to do so, because the court may not have the necessary equipment, and
>
> (b) provide the other party with a copy of the video or the opportunity to see it at least … days before the hearing.

In principle, no later than 28 days after giving special directions, the court may consider what *further* directions are to be given (CPR 27.4(1)(c)). In practice, either *standard* directions will be *varied*, *special* directions will be *added*, and a *final* hearing will be ordered, or a *preliminary* hearing will be ordered.

i. Preliminary hearing

The court may order a preliminary hearing for consideration of the claim (CPR 27.4(d)).

Before doing so, the court *must* have regard to the desirability of *limiting the expense* that the parties will incur due to attending court (CPR 27.6(2)). The court will give the parties at least 14 days' notice of the hearing (CPR 27.6(3)).

A preliminary hearing may only be ordered in one of three circumstances (CPR 27.6(1)).

First, *special* directions are needed to ensure a *fair* hearing, and it appears necessary for a party to *attend* a hearing, so as to ensure that she *understands* what she must do to *comply* with the special directions. Secondly, to *dispose* of the claim on the basis that one of the parties has *no real prospect of success*. Thirdly, to enable the court to *strike out* a statement of case, or part thereof, on the basis that it *discloses no reasonable grounds* for bringing or defending the claim.

If all parties agree, the court may treat a *preliminary* hearing as the *final* hearing (CPR 27.6(4)).

At, or after, a preliminary hearing, the court will do three things (CPR 27.6(5)).

First, *fix the date* of the *final* hearing (if the court has not done so already), and give the parties at least 21 days' *notice* of the same, unless they accept less notice. Secondly, inform the parties of the *amount of time* allowed for the final hearing. Thirdly, give any *other* appropriate directions.

j. Hearing fee

Once a claim is allocated to a track, a hearing fee is payable, typically 28 days before the hearing date (see chapter 23(b)(ii)). If the action does not proceed on the *claim*, but merely on the *counterclaim*, the hearing fee is payable by the *defendant*.

k. Disposal without a hearing

In principle, if *all* parties agree, the claim *may* be disposed of without a hearing (CPR 27.10). In practice, this is rare. The court may *still* order a final hearing.

12. Preparation

Everyone prepares in their own way. The following are merely suggestions. With experience, rituals of preparation often mature, with the consequent benefit of increasing time-efficiency, and effectiveness.

There are some universal rules, however, when preparing for a final hearing: promptly check that you have all of the papers; have at least one, spare, unmarked, hard copy of the papers; and consider the relevant information and documentation checklist.

a. Contact

The initial contact is likely to be a professional client calling or emailing a barristers' chambers, seeking to book counsel for representation. The professional client will speak to a barristers' "clerk"; the modern term for which is increasingly "practice manager". Sometimes, the professional client will know who they want to instruct, on other occasions however, they want a recommendation. If so, practice managers put forward counsel who are able to accept instructions.

If the names of those barristers are not known to the professional client, their names are likely (so I am told) to be typed into an online search engine before making a selection. This is one reason that it is important to keep online, professional profiles up to date with, for example, areas of practice, recent instructions, publications, training and seminars.

The practice manager will request that the professional client send whatever *papers* there are, agree a *fee*, and book the case into the selected barrister's professional *diary*. The papers, often sent by email, are printed off by the practice manager, and left in the barrister's pigeonhole. Counsel is then notified, so that she can *scan* the papers *promptly*.

b. Scan

Upon receipt of the papers, scan through them. Should any appear to be *missing*, *un*readable, or *breach* any applicable rules, practice directions, or court orders, those instructing should be put on *notice*, and *in plenty of time*, so that *they* are able to act *promptly*.

Check that the papers contain five types of documents.

First, *written* instructions. Secondly, statements of case. Thirdly, evidence. Fourthly, court *orders*. Fifthly, relevant *correspondence*, including *pre-action*, evidence of *filing* and *service*, *offers* of settlement, and *interim payments*.

The papers should include all of the documents that the written instructions say that they contain. Often, a bundle has *not* been agreed, so that the *claimant's* documents will be *separate* to those of the *defendant*. Ensure that you have *both* parties' papers.

i. Instructions

It is *always* preferable to have *written* instructions.

The professional client will often have drafted the case, corresponded with any witnesses, and have a view on the issues in dispute, merits, and compliance with rules, practice directions, and court orders.

Where there are no written instructions, at a *minimum*: a telephone call should be made to the professional client, so as to take *oral* instructions; and *confirm* them in *writing*, through an *email* to the professional client. The email may begin: 'Further to our telephone conversation this afternoon, just to put in writing your instructions …'.

Written instructions are often in a similar format, so that they can be marshalled into nine headings.

1. Enclosures

First, instructions state the *papers* that are enclosed.

This is likely to include a bundle for the final hearing (if there is one). Otherwise, there may be two bundles, or just a collection of papers on which both parties seek to rely.

Any relevant correspondence should also be included, such as *offers* to settle. If not apparent, telephone your professional client, so as to enquire *whether* or not an offer to settle has been made, and, if so, *when*, the *terms* thereof, and whether a *response* has been received.

2. Clients

Secondly, instructions state the *name* of your *professional* client, their firm, and the other party's professional client (if they are represented).

Instructions state the name of the party that you are instructed to represent (your lay client), whether the hearing is an application, or a final hearing, and the name of the court, date, and time that the hearing has been listed (if it is not on a floating list).

The time estimate for the hearing will often be provided (which can range from an hour and a half, up to a day). If it appears to be wholly inaccurate, advise your professional client, so that your professional client can notify the other party, and the court.

3. Facts

Thirdly, instructions set out the *material* facts of the case.

For example: 'The claim arises out of a road traffic collision, which took place on 15 September 2019'. If there is a *counter*claim, it should be noted. Whether liability, quantum, or both, are disputed should be apparent. The *heads of loss* that are claimed, the *sums* for each, and whether any *interest* is claimed should also be stated.

4. Issues

Fourthly, instructions confirm the *issues* in dispute.

Often, the particulars of claim include heads of loss that *the court* cannot award. For example, in a claim for credit hire, interest on special damages that have not already been paid.

The defence may deny each and every allegation, putting the claimant to strict proof, and requiring the claimant to provide, for example, a repair estimate, evidence of impecuniosity, and a credit hire agreement.

If the claimant provides this evidence, the defendant may accept the cost of repairs, and the sum claimed under the credit hire agreement. If so, these issues will no longer be in dispute. Accordingly, the issues in your *instructions* are likely to differ to those in the *statements of case*.

5. Authority

Fifthly, instructions confirm the name of any *authority* that is relied on, including (ideally) the neutral *citation*, where it is found in the *law reports*, and the *relevant* paragraph(s).

This authority may even be included in the papers (if so, check that it is the most authoritative law report, in accordance with chapter 13(b)).

Check whether there is any *additional* authority pleaded in the *statements of case*. If so, and you are unfamiliar with it, become familiar with the material point(s) of law for which it is authority for. You may need to print out sufficient copies for the court, the other party, and yourself, so that you are able to rely on it in the hearing.

6. Costs

Sixthly, instructions set out what *costs* are claimed.

Are there instructions to make an application for costs on the basis that the other party has behaved unreasonably? If so, what is the factual basis of the application?

Is there a witness statement in support? If not, and your professional view is that one would be of assistance, is there enough time for your professional client to settle one?

7. Offers

Seventhly, instructions confirm what *offers* have been made (if any), *when*, and *what* were they for?

Of course, the correspondence enclosing the offer, and the offer itself *should* be in the papers. If not, telephone your professional client, and request them.

8. Interim payments

Eighthly, instructions confirm whether any *interim payments* have been made, *when*, *by* whom, *to* whom, and for *how much*. If there was an interim payment, it may be acknowledged in the defence. Ideally, it should also be acknowledged in the particulars of claim.

9. Contact details

Ninthly, instructions confirm the *name, email* address, and *telephone number* of your *professional* client.

If she is out of the office for any period of time, this should be stated, along with the person to contact in her absence. If there are no such details, your practice manager should be able to assist.

ii. Statements of case

Statements of case should comply with rules, practice directions, and court orders. The correct names of the parties must also be used, in accordance with the same.

1. Compliant

Check that the statements of case conform to the relevant rules, practice directions, and court orders (see chapters 5-9 and 11). In particular, check that they contain a *valid* statement of truth.

2. Names

Also check that the *names of the parties* on the statements of case are correct.

Ensure that you have *written* instructions before making an *oral* application for permission, so as to *amend* the name on the *statements of case*, and to *dispense* with service.

For example, if the claimant has a contract with a *limited* company, but the name of the defendant on the claim form and particulars of claim does not end with 'limited', then, an application to amend should be made.

The relevant pages on the website of Companies House can be used to evidence the fact that a company is limited, as well as the company number. These should be printed, and copies brought to the hearing for the judge, and the other party.

iii. Evidence

More often than not, whatever point you wish to make can be made with the evidence that is *in* the papers.

Sometimes, however, you may need to weigh up the benefit of relying on an *objective*, *public* document, from a *reputable* source, against the likelihood that the other party, or the judge, will object to adducing it. In any event, when in doubt, speak to your professional client. Ensure that you act with instructions.

1. In the papers

The papers that you receive may not be arranged in the usual way.

That is, statements of case, evidence, and correspondence. There may be no rhyme or reason as to the ordering. If so, make sure that you do not miss, for example, a reply to the defence. There may be a reference to this statement of case in your instructions, or elsewhere in the papers.

The papers may not be paginated. If there are page numbers, they may not be continuous. Or, if there are separate papers for the claimant and the defendant, a document may appear at page ten of the former, and page one of the latter.

If an original document was *double*-sided, the copy may be *single*-sided, so that the version that you have is *missing* every other page. Photocopies of written, or even typed documents, may be impossible to read, truncated, or cropped. Photographs may be in black and white, so that they are of little, or even no, assistance.

Not all papers necessarily will be relevant. Especially this holds true with correspondence. Often, all correspondence relating to a case will be included, which can appear disproportionate to the issues that are in dispute.

Important correspondence includes evidence of *filing*, *service*, and *offers* to settle. Ensure that you have the same before the hearing.

2. Not in the papers

In a claim following a road traffic collision, for example, where there are no photographs, maps, or other images, of the road layout, the same are likely to assist the court. As such, the other party is unlikely to resist these being adduced, provided that the following conditions are satisfied.

First, *that party*, and *the court* are provided with copies *before* the hearing. Secondly, you *explain* to the other party, *and* to the court, *what* it is, *where* it is from, and the *good reason that it assists the court*. Thirdly, it is from an *objective, public, freely available* source. For example, Google Maps.

In the unlikely event that the accuracy of a piece of evidence can be rebutted using, for example, a printout from the website of Companies House, the other party is unlikely to agree to you being allowed to rely on it.

The court, on the other hand, may well allow it to adduce it, as the *strict* rules of evidence do *not* apply, and having balanced the factors that further the *overriding objective*, including that the case is dealt with *fairly*. In any event, the above three conditions should be satisfied.

iv. Orders

Court orders are necessary to confirm whether or not the parties have complied with the directions for the final hearing.

Whether or not the date for filing and service of witness statements has been complied with, for example; and, if not, the reason why. Fore-*warned* is often fore*armed*.

It is preferable to give a party *some* notice of a document, as opposed to *no notice whatsoever*.

If the other party has had a day or so to consider it, and to take instructions, although it is likely to fall foul of standard directions – including, to deliver all documents on which a party intends to rely no later than 14 days before the final hearing – the prejudice of excluding that evidence will have to be weighed against the prejudice of admitting it. That balance is likely to change *materially*, even if the innocent party has had only *one* days' notice.

v. Correspondence

Correspondence falls under four sub-headings.

First, *pre*-action. Secondly, evidence of *filing* and *service*. Thirdly, *offers* of settlement. Fourthly, evidence of any *interim payments*.

1. Pre-action

Pre-action correspondence is important for the purpose of deciding costs (see chapters 23(a)(i)(1) and 24(c)(i)).

2. Filing & serving

Especially on an unassigned list, or where a claim has been transferred from one court to another, you should have evidence of filing and service.

All too often, the same is disputed. With *evidence* of the same, you help the court to further the overriding objective by dealing with the case *expeditiously*, and *fairly*. Disputes relating to filing and service may be determined with the evidence of the same *swiftly*.

3. Offers

Offers of settlement, and any associated replies, are important for two reasons.

First, if an offer remains *open for acceptance*, there may have been a material change in circumstances since the offer was made – for example, a *key* witness is no longer able to attend the final hearing – so that it is *now* advisable to accept that offer. Secondly, offers are relevant when deciding what order for costs (if any) to make (see chapters 23(a)(i)(3) and 24(c)(iv)(3)(a)).

4. Interim payments

If there has been an interim payment, and it is not acknowledged in a statement of case, you should have evidence of that interim payment. If there is no evidence, and the other party does not accept that there has been an interim payment, then, you can invite the court to add a paragraph into the order, providing that credit is to be given for any sums already paid.

c. Analyse

Having confirmed that you have written instructions, statements of case, and evidence, a careful reading will enable you to confirm for yourself the *relevant* issues, facts, and law.

A black pen or a highlighter can be used to mark the salient parts of the written instructions.

The facts in the evidence on which you must cross-examine may also be usefully emphasised. Marking often assists to recall relevant facts, over and above reading alone. Evidence can be highlighted, underlined, or a vertical line can be drawn down the margin of a significant passage of text.

i. Agreed facts

Having carefully read the papers, it should be possible to identify the *material* facts that are not in dispute.

In a claim for an unpaid parking charge, for example, it may be possible to make a note that the following are agreed facts.

First, the defendant parked on the relevant land. Secondly, she did so for the time alleged by the claimant. Thirdly, the defendant was obliged to pay. Fourthly, the claimant was responsible for the management of the relevant land.

Agreed facts are *important*.

They are the *anchor* from which the judge can build a picture as to what happened. From this, you must construct your client's case, using the evidence that *is* in dispute, so as to persuade the court that the claimant has discharged the burden of proof, or not, depending on the party that you are representing.

ii. Disputed facts

Having noted the facts that are *not* in dispute, it should be possible to identify the facts that *are* in dispute, relevant, and therefore assist, or undermine, one of the conflicting cases.

For example, in that claim for an unpaid parking charge:

First, the sign notifying the defendant that payment was required was clear / confusing. Secondly, there was / was not a way to make the payment, as the payment machine was / was not working. Thirdly, in these circumstances, the sum claimed is / is not excessive.

If the likelihood of each of the conflicting cases are finely balanced, then, the burden of proof can effectively be deployed. A defendant can use it successfully to argue that the claim should be dismissed.

If there is a claim, *and* a *counter*claim following the same incident, however, the burden of proof is of less assistance, as the *claimant* has the burden of proving the *claim*, and the *defendant* has the burden of proving the *counter*claim. As such, *both* parties have a burden.

iii. Issues

Having carefully read the papers, it should be possible to identify the *real* issues in the case.

These are often more discrete than the statements of cases suggest. Once an issue has been identified, the opposing positions taken on that issue in the statements of case can be identified. Then, the disputed evidence which goes to that issue can be considered.

This informs cross-examination, as there is no need to ask questions that go to issues which are not in dispute.

d. Checklist of information & documents

Depending on the type of case, the court usually needs certain information and documentation (PD 27 at Appendix A).

i. Road traffic

First, witness statements (including statements from the parties themselves). Secondly, invoices and estimates for repairs. Thirdly, agreements and invoices for the cost of any car hire.

Fourthly, the police accident report. Fifthly, a sketch plan, which should, wherever possible, be agreed. Sixthly, photographs of the scene of the accident, and photographs of the damage.

ii. Building, repairs, goods sold & contract

First, any written contract. Secondly, photographs. Thirdly, any plans. Fourthly, a list of works complained of. Fifthly, a list of any outstanding works.

Sixthly, any relevant estimate, invoice, or receipt, including any relating to repairs to each of the defects. Seventhly, invoices for work done or goods supplied. Eighthly, estimates for work to be completed. Ninthly, a valuation of work done to date.

iii. Landlord & tenant

First, a calculation of the amount of any rent alleged to be owing, showing amounts received, preferably in the form of a schedule. Secondly, details of breaches of an agreement which are said to justify withholding any deposit itemised, showing how the total is made up, with invoices and estimates in support.

iv. Breach of duty

First, what it is said by the claimant that is alleged to have been done negligently by the defendant. Secondly, why it is said that this negligence is the fault of the defendant. Thirdly, what damage is said to have been caused.

Fourthly, what injury, or what losses have been suffered, and how any (and each) sum that is claimed has been calculated. Fifthly, the response of the defendant to each of the above.

e. Telephone

If a document appears to be missing, evidence appears not to have conformed to the rules, practice directions, or court's directions, or you just wish to touch base before the day of the hearing, *speak to your professional client* over the telephone.

There may be important context that has not made its way into your written instructions, perhaps due to time constraints. Your professional client may feel more at ease having confirmation that her selected barrister has received the papers, understands the instructions, and is grateful for them – especially if it is the first time that she has instructed you.

f. Spare copies

Take a spare, hard, unmarked, colour copy of the papers to the hearing.

This is because the court directions will not usually state which party is responsible for providing a witness bundle. All too often, the papers are filed with the court, and served on the other side, but the court, *and* the other side, are missing *key* (and sometimes *most* of the) papers.

13. Authority

Lord Justice Lewison recently opined in *Parr v Keystone Healthcare Ltd & Ors* [2019] EWCA Civ 1246, [2019] 4 WLR 99 at [26], that "it is a matter of considerable regret that the practice direction on the citation of authorities … has been almost wholly ignored."

Even in an appellate court, then, authorities are relied upon other than in accordance with the guidance that the court has given. Whether you are in the Court of Appeal, or the county court, you are under an obligation to help the court to further the overriding objective when relying on authority.

a. Legal principle

Lord Justice Floyd recently endorsed a warning in a patent case, issued well over one hundred years ago. It appears that it is incapable of improvement (*Kaur & Anor v Secretary of State for the Home Department* [2019] EWCA Civ 1101, [2019] 4 WLR 94 at [48]):

> "Cases, so far as regards the law, are most useful, but when they are applied to particular facts, they, as a rule, are of little service. Each case depends on its own particular facts, and the facts of almost every case differ …"

The lesson is that, as a general rule, authorities should be relied on for a statement of *legal principle*. A previous case is unlikely to be so factually similar that it can be relied on, so as to bind a (deputy) district judge, hearing a claim that is allocated to the small claims track.

Most such claims are decided on the facts, after the benefit of oral evidence, so that it is *unlikely* that such an authority is capable of identification in advance of a final hearing.

b. Practice Direction (Citation of Authorities) [2012] 1 WLR 780

In 2012, the then Lord Chief Justice issued the *Practice Direction (Citation of Authorities)* [2012] 1 WLR 780.

The preamble provides that it was "issued in order to clarify the practice and procedure governing the citation of authorities and applies throughout the ... county courts". Under the heading 'Citation of authority', it prescribes that: "When authority is cited, whether in written or oral submissions, the following practice should be followed."

i. Official Law Reports

Where a judgment is reported in any of the four, *official* Law Reports ("the Law Reports"), *that* report *must* be cited: 1) Appeal Cases ("AC"); 2) Queen's Bench ("QB"); 3) Chancery ("Ch"); 4) Family ("Fam"). This is for two reasons.

First, these are the *most* authoritative. Secondly, they contain a *summary* of the *arguments*.

ii. Weekly Law Reports & All England Law Reports

Until a case is reported in the Law Reports, if it is reported in the Weekly Law Reports ("WLR"), or it is reported in the All England Law Reports ("All ER"), the WLR or the All ER *should* be cited. There is no hierarchy. Either may be used.

iii. Specialist series

If three conditions are satisfied, a specialist report may be cited.

First, the case is *not* reported in the Law Reports, WLR, or All ER. Secondly, it contains a *headnote*. Thirdly, it was made by individuals holding a *senior courts qualification*.

iv. Other reports

Only when a case is not reported in any of the above may other reports be cited.

v. Transcripts

Only when a case has not been reported in *any* report may the official transcript be used.

This may be found on the website of the British and Irish Legal Information Institute (www.bailii.org). An *un*reported case should *not* be cited usually, "unless it contains a relevant statement of legal principle not found in reported authority."

vi. Format

Regardless of which law reports are relied on, an authority must be in one of two formats.

First, a photocopy of the published report. Secondly, a copy of a reproduction of the case in electronic form, which has been authorised by the publisher of the relevant reports.

In any event, it must be easily legible, ideally with a 12-point font.

c. Practice Direction (Citation of Authorities) [2001] 1 WLR 1001

With the substantial growth in the number of cases that are available, reported in (sometimes a number of different) law reports, and transcripts that are freely available online, the court has limited the *nature,* and the *amount,* of authority that may be relied upon.

This drive to increase *efficiency* and *proportionality* of litigation, so as to reduce its *cost*, both to the *parties*, and to the *court*, must be *balanced* against the *interests of justice*. It is in conformity with the *overriding objective* to deal with cases in ways that are *proportionate*.

Accordingly, in 2001, the then Lord Chief Justice issued the *Practice Direction (Citation of Authorities)* [2001] 1 WLR 1001, prescribing three rules that apply to claims that are allocated to the small claims track.

i. Relevant & useful

The overriding objective will be compromised if the court is burdened with a weight of *in*appropriate, *un*necessary authority, and advocates are *un*certain as to the extent to which it is necessary to use authority.

Accordingly, this practice direction limits citation of authority to cases that are both *relevant,* and that are *useful to the court*. The caveat that it must be *useful to the court* is a reference to the duty to cite authority that goes *against* the case that you are advancing.

ii. Adverse authority

An advocate is under a duty to draw the court's attention to authority that *undermines* the case that she is advancing, and that has *not* been cited by the other party.

In the context of a claim for credit hire, for example, where enforceability is in dispute, this may include *Irving v Morgan Sindall Plc* [2018] EWHC 1147 (QB), [2018] RTR 23. In this case, it was held that the claimant, who had been assured by a credit hire company that she would never be personally responsible for hire charges, had a *contingent* liability to the hire company, so that she was *not* getting a free hire car, and the defendant *was* liable to pay these charges.

iii. County court authority

A county court case may *not* be cited *unless* it clearly indicates that *it purports to establish a new principle*, or to *extend* the present law. This indication *must* be in the form of an *express statement* to that effect. There are two exceptions.

First, to illustrate the conventional measure of damages in a *personal injury* case. Secondly, to demonstrate current, county court authority, on an issue where there is *no* higher-level authority.

In practice, then, before relying on county court authority, you should be able positively to submit that there is no binding (High Court, Court of Appeal, or Supreme Court) authority on the point.

d. Citation

When a case is cited, the full case name should be used.

When written, *italics* should be used for the *names* of the parties. This should be followed by the *neutral* citation (if there is one), a comma, followed by where it is cited in the *most* authoritative law reports.

When a particular paragraph is cited, the number of that paragraph can be encompassed within square brackets. For example: *Barton v Wright Hassal LLP* [2018] UKSC 12, [2018] 3 All ER 487 at [18].

e. Marked

The relevant paragraph(s) can be marked. Black pen should be used, so that, where the authority is scanned, or photocopied, it remains legible. A vertical, straight line can be drawn down the side of the page encompassing the relevant sentence(s), or paragraph(s).

f. Spare copies

Once an authority is printed, and marked, it can be photocopied, thereby saving time in marking up each, individual copy. This also ensures that *all* copies are *identical* to the *original*.

The judge should be provided with a hard copy of any authority that is relied on. Before the hearing, after signing in with the usher, the authority should be handed to that usher, so that it can be passed to the judge.

Any document which is provided to the *court* must *also* be provided to the other *party*. This should be as soon as practicable, so that there is as much time as possible for the other party to consider it. Both the legal principle that decided the case, and the relevant paragraph(s), should be communicated to the other party.

You will need a copy, too. If you are content with an electronic copy, the original can be scanned, and emailed to your professional email address. Otherwise, if you write on your hard copy, make a note on the front of it, so that you don't mistakenly hand it to the court, or to another party.

g. Cost / benefit

Claims that are allocated to the small claims track are usually determined by findings of fact.

The relevant legal principles are usually trite. Accordingly, use of authorities should be the exception, *not* the norm.

If you are aware that the other side is not represented, carefully balance the benefit of relying on an authority, against the (perhaps unwarranted) perception that you are browbeating a litigant in person. In any event, beware not to court the ire of the judge, who may not wish to read a lengthy, appellate analysis, bearing on trite law.

h. Context

Using a professional legal database, check for three *material* circumstances before deciding to rely on an authority.

First, whether or not it has been positively considered in *later* cases. Secondly, whether or not it has been successfully *appealed*. Thirdly, whether or not it is subject to a *pending* appeal.

If the answer to any of these questions is "yes", then, this *must* be communicated, both to the other *party*, and to the *court*.

i. Subsequent consideration

If the legal principle that decided a case has been *applied* to *decide* a later case, this is likely to indicate that it is *good* law. Especially if the latter is an *appellate* court, the paragraph that you rely on is cited *word-for-word*, or the reasoning behind that principle is approved by *express* words. It may *also* indicate, however, that the legal principle is trite, thereby calling into question whether it is necessary to cite authority in support of that principle at all.

It should be obvious that, if a case has been *negatively* considered, *criticised*, or *confined to its facts*, especially by a *higher* court, this *weakens* any general authority that it may have. These facts would need to be disclosed to the court, and to the other party. It follows that, on balance, a weak, or a questionable authority, may not be worth relying on.

ii. Determined appeal

If the case on which you seek to rely has been appealed, check for three material circumstances.

First, whether or not the appeal was *successful*. Secondly, whether or not the legal point that you seek to rely on was *endorsed*. Thirdly, whether or not the *reasoning* of the lower court applying that principle was endorsed.

To take one example, in *Stevens v Equity Syndicate Management Ltd* [2014] EWHC 689 (QB), [2014] RTR 34 at [21], Mr Justice Burnett (as he then was) held that the trial judge had been entitled to find that the claimant was not impecunious in these terms:

> "It is striking that the bank statements showed very little activity at all. In other words, the money passing through the bank account could not conceivably reflect the totality of economic activity of a man, still less a family man. …"

On appeal, Lord Justice Kitchin (as he then was, with which Floyd and Jackson LJJ agreed) said: "Burnett J upheld the Recorder's findings on impecuniosity and there is no further appeal against that decision" ([2015] EWCA Civ 93, [2015] 4 All ER 458 at [7]).

Accordingly, the decision of Mr Justice Burnett was appealed, *but not on the grounds of his judgment on impecuniosity*. The above reasoning on impecuniosity, then, remains good law.

It was *not* expressly endorsed by the Court of Appeal, however, as High Court authority binds a (deputy) district judge, recorder, and circuit judge, this is of *no* consequence to the final hearing of a claim that has been allocated to the small claims track.

iii. Pending appeal

If there is an *application* for permission to appeal, or permission to appeal has been *granted*, this is a relevant fact that should be *stated* to the other *party*, and to the *court*.

Potentially, these circumstances *weaken* the authority upon which you intend to rely, as there is a *prospect* that the judgment will be *reversed*, the legal principle upon which you intend to rely will be *criticised*, or *different* reasoning surrounding the principle will be endorsed.

Accordingly, the benefit of relying on such an authority should be carefully considered.

14. Skeleton arguments

The purpose of a skeleton argument 'is to assist the court by setting out as concisely as practicable the arguments upon which a party intends to rely' (PD 52A at [5.1(1)]).

a. Assist the court

Skeleton arguments are usually not necessary in claims that are allocated to the small claims track. Often, the issues are obvious. The applicable law is trite. The facts are straightforward.

Frequently, a claim that is allocated to the small claims track turns on *oral* evidence, which can*not* be anticipated in writing before the hearing.

Where instructed to make an application to strike out a statement of case because it is an abuse of process, however, a skeleton argument *is* likely to *assist the court* in setting out the *key* facts, legal principles, and submissions.

Skeleton arguments also provide an opportunity to get the judge onboard with your arguments *before* you open your mouth.

b. Requirements

There are six requirements of a skeleton argument (PD 52A at [5.1(2)]).

First, *concision*. Secondly, *de*fine and *con*fine areas of controversy. Thirdly, *numbered* paragraphs and pages. Fourthly, cross-reference relevant documents. Fifthly, be *self*-contained. Sixthly, *omit* extensive quotations.

i. Concision

Words, sentences, and paragraphs should be *short*.

Headings, sub-headings, and lists can be used for ease of *navigation*, *organising* content, and *reducing* word count.

Skeleton arguments before *substantive appeals* in the *Court of Appeal* should be less than *25* pages. Accordingly, in a *claim* that is allocated to the *small claims* track, there should be a *very* good reason to go beyond, say, *ten* pages.

1. Headings & sub-headings

Typical headings may include *facts*, *issues*, and *submissions*.

Sub-headings can also be used to make arguments.

Where resisting an application for relief from sanctions, for example, under the heading 'submissions', sub-headings may include: 1) breach is serious and significant; 2) no good reason; and 3) all the circumstances weigh in favour of refusing relief.

2. Lists & punctuation

Lists enable *brevity*, by reducing the number of words that are necessary to convey information.

Punctuation, too, can aid both *pithiness*, and *clarity*. This includes appropriate use of the Oxford comma; semi-colons to separate two, closely related, but independent sentences; and full colons before a list, or where a semi-colon will not do. Paragraphs should be *short*.

3. Layout

Concision does *not* mean that the font, size of font, and space in between each line should be reduced, so as to cram more content onto each side of a page.

On the contrary, content should be *well*-spaced, so that it is *clear*, and *notes* can be written in the *margins*, and *in between* sentences. Typically, Times New Roman, font size 12, and 1.5-line spacing is used.

ii. Define & confine areas of controversy

Both the issues that *are* in dispute, and the issues that are *not* in dispute, should be identified, and the *scope* thereof set out. In a claim for credit hire, for example: 'Liability is accepted. Quantum is in issue. In particular, need, and period.'

iii. Numbering

Pages *and* paragraphs should be numbered, for ease of navigation.

There are at least two advantages to *single*-sided skeleton arguments.

First, there are *blank* pages, so that *lengthy* notes may be written on *these* pages, where there is insufficient space in the margin, or in-between lines. Secondly, should the skeleton argument need to be photocopied, or scanned, there is a greater prospect that *all* of the pages will, in fact, be photocopied, or scanned.

iv. Cross-referencing

Where an *admission* in a statement of case, or a piece of *evidence* is relied on, for example, the *name* of the document, and *where it is found* should be identified, as precisely as possible.

Often, a *paginated* bundle does *not* exist. If so, 'paragraph 7 of the Defence', or 'page 2 of the claimant's engineers report', for example, provide workarounds.

Authority should be relied upon in accordance with the practice directions issued by court (see chapter 13(a) and (b)). Where it is necessary to rely on an authority, it can aid concision to set out the following.

First, the *legal principle* for which it is authority. Secondly, the *paragraph(s)* of the authority where it is found. Thirdly, if *more* than one authority is relied on to establish this principle, the *reason* why. For example:

1. When a claim is issued, a claimant must bring forward her whole case. She can*not* subsequently open the same litigation in respect of matters which ought to have been brought forward, but, in fact, were not.

2. This is "Henderson abuse". It has been well-established law since Wigram V-C set out the rule in the case of *Henderson v Henderson* [1843-60] All ER Rep 378 at 381, in these terms:

    "… where a given matter becomes the subject of litigation in, and of adjudication by, a court of competent jurisdiction, the court requires the parties to that litigation to bring forward their whole case, and will not (except under special circumstances) permit the same parties to open the same subject of litigation in respect of matter which might have been brought forward as part of the subject in contest, but which was not brought forward only because they have, from negligence, inadvertence, or even accident, omitted part of their case. …"

Adopt a *consistent* shorthand for referring to page and paragraph numbers, and *state* what that is. For example: 'References in square brackets are to paragraph numbers.' If so, be careful not to use square brackets for page numbers also.

v. Self-contained

The *key* submissions should be set out.

A skeleton argument that is *not* self-contained may state that, for example: 'the first submission is set out in paragraph four of the Defence'; 'the second submission appears in paragraph twelve of the Defence'; and 'the third submission can be found on page 67 of the bundle'.

Footnotes should not be required.

vi. Quotations

As a general rule, only the *key* sentence should be quoted.

Occasionally, there will be more than one key sentence. There should be a very good reason to quote more than a paragraph. If there is, it may be worth briefly setting out, so as to allay the judge's wrath in advance.

Do not quote out of any *material* context.

c. Content

Skeleton arguments – like particulars of claim, defences, and opinions – have few strict rules. There is flexibility to find your own style. What follows, therefore, are merely general rules, conventions, and suggestions.

i. Headings

The top of the first page of a skeleton argument should appear much the same as that of statements of case (see chapter 5(b)(ii)).

The sole exception is, of course, the *title* of the document. This should also be within tramlines, capitalised, and emboldened, but, in contrast to a statement of case, it should start with the status of the party, followed by the name of the document. If it relates to an application, the name of the application can be used.

For example: **'DEFENDANT'S SKELETON ARGUMENT RE ABUSE OF PROCESS'**.

ii. Reading time

An estimate of the amount of *time* that it takes to *read* should follow the heading.

This enables the court to gauge how long it will take to consider the skeleton argument, and thereby fulfil the duty actively to case-manage, by controlling the progress of the case. It is hard to envisage a skeleton argument in a claim that is allocated to the small claims track with a reading time of more than 10-15 minutes.

iii. Invitation

In a sentence, set out *what* the court is being asked to do.

For example: 'The court is invited to strike out this claim as an abuse of process under CPR 3.4(2)(b) because there is a binding settlement.'

If there is a *relevant* CPR, practice direction, or court order, *cite it*, stating under what power you are inviting the court to act.

iv. Facts

Set out only the *necessary* facts.

In a skeleton argument inviting the court to strike out a case as it is an abuse of process, for example, the salient facts may be as follows:

1. This claim arises out of a road traffic collision, which occurred on 10 July 2019.

2. Liability is not in dispute.

3. On 12 August 2019, the claimant submitted a Claim Notification Form ("CNF") under the MOJ Portal ("the Portal").

4. Section E of the CNF was completed, relating to provision of an alternative vehicle. The claimant indicated that she required an alternative vehicle, but also that she had not been provided with one. No details of hire were provided.

5. No request was made to the defendant insurer to provide an alternative vehicle.

6. From 5-20 August 2019, the claimant hired a vehicle on credit hire terms.

7. On 29 October 2019, the claimant submitted the Stage 2 Settlement Pack, claiming personal injury, and physiotherapy charges.

8. On 12 November 2019, the defendant made a final offer of £3,500. On 3 December 2019, this was accepted.

9. On 4 February 2020, proceedings were issued against the defendant to recover the following:

    a) credit hire in the sum of £4,545.53; and
    b) repairs, in the sum of £4,210.12.

10. This was two months after settlement.

v. Costs

If costs are sought because the other party has behaved unreasonably, *say* so. For example:

> If the court strikes out this claim as an abuse of process, it follows that the claimant has behaved unreasonably in bringing this claim for the purposes of CPR 27.14(2)(g). Accordingly, the defendant invites the court to award the reasonable cost of defending this matter, set out in the Defendant's Statement of Costs.

vi. Sign & date

The name of the person who has drafted a skeleton argument should appear at the bottom.

By convention, it is capitalised, emboldened, and aligned to the right-hand side of the page. The date should also appear on the bottom. These are the last words before the back sheet.

vii. Back sheet

Skeleton arguments usually have a back sheet, with the same heading as the first page, but with text on the right-hand side of the page only.

In addition, the name, address, and status of *counsel* who has settled the skeleton argument (for example, counsel for the defendant) should be provided; as well as the name, address, and status of the legal representative *instructing* counsel (for example, solicitor for the defendant).

If printed off and stapled, the *back* sheet should face the *back*. This is so that, when the skeleton argument is picked up, you can see the front page, and, when you turn the skeleton argument over, you can see the back sheet, for ease of reference.

viii. Spelling, grammar & punctuation

Poor spelling, grammar, and punctuation, all indicate that the necessary time has not been invested in researching, writing, and proofreading.

Accordingly, the ability to persuade will diminish. The judge is likely to have formed a negative view of your client's case, you, your arguments, or all three, *before you have even opened your mouth.*

d. Form

Substance is important. But so is *form*.

A skeleton argument should look aesthetically pleasing.

This demonstrates that time has been invested in *proofreading*, so as to ensure that *text* is all the *same* font and size, *spacing* is *consistent*, and *shorthand* is used *consistently*.

For example: 'paragraph 4', 'para. 4', or '[4]'; and 'Particulars of Claim', 'PoC', or 'particulars of claim'.

Before using an abbreviation, define it. By convention, this is done by brackets and quotation marks ("…").

e. Notice

If there is a *need* for a skeleton argument, the *facts*, *law*, *submissions*, or some *combination* thereof, is likely to be *complicated*.

Accordingly, the *judge*, and the other *party*, should have sufficient *notice*, so as to *read*, *process*, and, if they wish, conduct their *own* research into the points raised by your skeleton argument.

If a party has *sufficient* notice of your submissions, and yet, has still *not* been able to counter them *effectively*, they become all the more powerful. It follows that the court is *more* likely to exercise a *draconian* power of case-management, such as *strike out* a statement of case, or grant *summary judgment* disposing of a claim or defence.

i. File & serve

Ideally, skeleton arguments should be filed and served no less than three days before a hearing.

Some notice is better than *no* notice at all, however, so, if the skeleton argument is filed and served the afternoon before the hearing, this *is* preferable to not filing or serving it at all.

Ensure that you have emails or covering letters at the hearing, evidencing that the skeleton argument *has* been filed and served, in case there is a dispute over the same.

ii. Springboard

Skeleton arguments are not statements of case, or evidence, however, so, if they have not been filed or served, and *the court* will not read it, *you* can.

Of course, if you read it word-for-word, the judge may be inclined to find a reason to find against your client, so do not use it as a script, but, rather, as a *springboard* into your submissions, the law, and the evidence.

15. Arrival

On arrival at court, *sign in* with the usher, have a *conference* with your client and any witnesses for the party that you represent, and have a *discussion* with the other party.

If the usher invites you to do so, complete a case management form.

There are no separate courts, buildings, or rooms, notwithstanding the phrase "small claims court". Claims that are allocated to the small claims track, fast track, and multi-track, are all held in the *same* courts, buildings, and rooms.

a. Sign in

When you arrive at court, *sign in with the usher*. There are three reasons for doing so.

First, so that the hearing will *not* proceed without you. Secondly, so that, if you have any *witnesses*, when they sign in, the usher will be able to inform *them* that you are at court, so that you can promptly have a conference. Thirdly, so that, when the *other party* signs in, the usher will be able to inform them that *you* are at court, so as to speak to them.

b. Note

Before the hearing, take a note of the courtroom that the matter will be heard in. This is so that you do not forget to do so after the hearing; and, in case of an appeal, where a transcript of the hearing may be requested.

Note the title – for example, (deputy) district judge – and the name of the judge that will hear the matter. If a legal representative for the other party has already signed in, take a note of their title (for example, Ms), and their name.

Your attendance note should include: the name of the court; courtroom that the matter was heard in; judge who sat in it; and the name of the legal representative of the other party (if there was one).

c. Listing

Most courts list many claims at 10:00, or at 14:00.

This does *not* mean that your case will be called *before*, or even *at*, this time. It means that *you must have signed in with the usher* before 10:00 or 14:00.

You may be waiting an hour, morning, or even an entire day before your case is adjourned due to lack of judicial time. If you think that this is a realistic prospect, you may wish to ensure that any of your witnesses are aware that this is a real possibility.

Your case may not have an assigned listing. That is, before the hearing, there may *not* be a *fixed* courtroom in which the matter will be heard, *judge* who will hear it, or even time before which the matter *will* be called on. If so, it is said to be on an "unassigned" (or "floating") list.

i. Managing expectations

If so, ensure that your witnesses are aware of this. Often, lay clients equate *listing* with a professional *appointment*. They may need to make childcare arrangements, renew their parking, or otherwise make additional arrangements. This can be explained in a conference.

ii. Spare copies

Where the matter is on a floating list, the prospects that the court will have all of the papers, and that a separate witness bundle has made its way to the correct court, are often *drastically* reduced. This is another reason why it is prudent to take *at least* one spare, unmarked, hard copy of the papers to any hearing, along with *evidence* of *filing* and *service*.

iii. County Court at Central London

In the County Court at Central London, when you sign in, you will be asked for your name, and, sometimes, a mobile telephone number.

When a *courtroom*, and a *judge* becomes available, the court will notify the parties. Sometimes, via text message. The parties will also be released for the luncheon adjournment by the same means. If you wish to speak to the other side, you can request a text message to be sent to them, inviting them to return to the reception area, so as to facilitate a discussion.

iv. Alternative dispute resolution

As you may be waiting around for some time, your duty to assist the court to further the overriding objective – so as to save the expense of the matter dragging on – requires you to *attempt* at least to *narrow*, if not in fact *settle*, the issues.

If you do not have authority to do so, telephone your professional client, request the same; and, if necessary, explain why it is a good use of time, as it will save the expense of further counsel' fees, should the matter be adjourned.

There may be an option to elect to use the Small Claims Mediation Service (see chapter 10(e)).

In practice, if both sides have legal representation, and instructed counsel, it may not be possible to ascertain authority to use this service. If this is the case, then, the corollary is that, with counsel, the parties should be able to narrow the issues to only those which are *properly* arguable.

It can be a sign of a *weak* point, with which counsel does not agree, but feels *obliged* to argue on *instructions*, when the phrase "let's let the judge decide" is used. This is likely to demonstrate that there is no good authority, or even a properly arguable argument.

Never agree with another party that a point you are taking is doomed to fail; if it is, drop it.

Whatever the other party thinks, and sometimes candidly says about their case, it is often useful to know in advance of the hearing. By doing so, you will learn more about *how* the other party will *pitch* their case, their *perceived* strengths, and, potentially, their *weaknesses*.

v. Subsequent listing

If your case is adjourned, be sure to request a *fixed* listing on the return date.

It will likely be granted. In any event, if you do not ask, you may not get.

d. Non-attendance of witnesses

If it appears as though a witness is not going to attend, *telephone* your professional client.

If you cannot get through to them, send them an *email*.

There may be a *good* reason that they have not attended. For example, they may have had to attend an accident and emergency department of a hospital. Instructions from your professional client, confirming the same, will often secure an adjournment, and defend against an application for costs on the basis that a party has behaved unreasonably (see chapter 24(c)(iv)(3)(b)).

It may be, *especially* where the matter has been *transferred* between courts, that a witness has gone to the *wrong* court. In any event, *act promptly*. Do not wait until the last minute to make the telephone call to your professional client.

e. Late attendance of legal representative

If you have reason to believe that *your* arrival at court will be tardy, again, act *promptly*.

First, send an *email* to your *professional* client, *copying in* your *practice manager*, stating that you are *likely* to be late, the *reason*, and your estimated *time* of arrival. Your professional client may email the other party to convey the same, especially if she is represented.

Secondly, request that your *practice manager email the court* to relay the same, copying you in. The court may have other matters in the list that can be dealt with before the one in which you are instructed.

Witnesses *will* be grateful to be kept informed. Court can be stressful enough without the prospect that their legal representative will apparently abandon them in their hour of need.

Above all, it is a professional courtesy. Trains are delayed, and even cancelled.

What matters is that the *delay*, the *reason* for that delay, and your likely arrival *time*, are communicated *promptly*.

f. Conference

If you are instructed in a claim where liability has been accepted, and the issues in dispute do not require oral evidence, you may not have a witness. In this case, there will be no one with whom to have a conference.

Especially where liability is in dispute, however, you will likely need a conference with your client, and any witness for the party that you represent (see chapter 16(c)).

g. Speak to the other party

There are five reasons to speak to the other party, ahead of the hearing.

First, confirm that each party has a copy of the relevant *papers*. Secondly, agree the *issues* that are in dispute. Thirdly, attempt to agree *quantum*, subject to liability. Fourthly, exchange *authority*. Fifthly, agree *costs and witness expenses*, subject to liability.

i. Papers

If a legal representative has not got a copy of a document that you seek to rely upon, you should be able to provide them with a copy. If they say that they have not seen the document before, or dispute that they have been served with a copy of it, speak to your professional client, and request evidence of *service* via email.

It is also worth requesting evidence that the document has been *filed* with the court, in case the court does not have a copy on file. Once received, evidence of service can be shown to the other party, so that these issues can be resolved before the hearing.

ii. Issues

In a credit hire dispute, if the claimant has served evidence of impecuniosity, the defendant may decide not to dispute that the claimant is, in fact, impecunious. This means that at least one, *significant* issue is no longer in dispute. The need to cross-examine a claimant on her current account statements, wage slips, and credit card statements falls away.

When relayed to the claimant before the hearing, this is likely to be reassuring.

For the defendant, too, there is reassurance in knowing where the real battleground lies.

It will also enable the parties to state the issues that *are* in dispute at the *outset* of the hearing, so as to *focus* evidence, and then submissions on the *real* issues, which may be *different*, or at least *narrower* than was previously the case.

iii. Quantum

If there is an invoice, subject to liability, it may be possible to agree the head of loss to which it relates. If so, again, this saves court time.

For a claimant, it can be reassuring to agree quantum subject to liability. If she succeeds on liability, a known amount will follow, without the uncertainty that would accompany leaving quantum to be decided by the court. The estimated length of the hearing may also reduce, so that, especially in an unassigned list, your case may be more likely to be called on.

If *quantum* can be agreed, subject to liability, then, in principle, so can *interest*, and the *period* for *payment*. For example, 21 days, where the court would otherwise order payment within 14 days.

iv. Authority

Any authority that you wish to rely on should be given to the other side *before* the hearing.

This *includes* rules of the *Highway Code*.

Do *not* assume that the other party is familiar with an authority, *even if* they indicate passively that they are. The *legal principle* for which it is authority, and the *paragraph* at which this is found, should *both* be clearly communicated to the other party.

This is even more important, as a matter of ethics, where the other party is *un*represented.

v. Costs, disbursements & witness expenses

Costs, disbursements, and witness expenses can usually be agreed before a hearing, subject to liability (see chapter 23(b), (c), and (d)). If witness expenses appear to be *un*reasonably high, the paying party may request to *cross-examine*, usually after judgment, when the issue of costs is being decided.

h. Case management form

Not all courts have a case management form to be completed before an application or final hearing. Those that do, often have *different*, bespoke forms; and so *different* questions, requiring *differing* amounts of detail.

Having *signed in*, had a *conference* with your client, and any witnesses, and confirmed the *issues in dispute* with the other party, you should be in a position to complete the case management form on behalf of the party who you represent.

This is likely to include, at a minimum: a time estimate for the hearing; identifying whether there are any applications to be made; and whether liability, quantum, or both, are in dispute.

16. Conference

Where liability is in dispute, a conference with at least one witness is often necessary.

Even where only quantum is in dispute, a witness may be needed to give evidence. For example, in a claim for credit hire, where the defendant wishes to cross-examine on the need to hire, or whether or not the claimant is impecunious. In these circumstances, a conference is vital for at least three reasons.

First, to build *rapport*. Secondly, to outline the *procedure* that the court is likely to follow. Third, confirm whether the *witness statement* is accurate.

a. Build rapport

For an effective conference, so as to fill in any gaps in the evidence time-efficiently, you need *rapidly* to build rapport. Having done so, the witness is more likely to have trust and confidence in you, and forthrightly answer any questions. You will then be in a position to advise, take instructions, and to represent the best interests of your client during a hearing.

i. Greeting

A *genuine* smile, *appropriate* eye contact, and a *sincere* greeting all assist to build rapport. Open body language can also help. Briefly introducing yourself often puts a witness at ease, as can stating that you have let the usher know that you are here, and that you will try to find a private room in which to hold a conference.

ii. Privacy

Finding a private conference room is often easier if you arrive early. In many county courts, there are a *very* limited number of conference rooms. If you are able to find one, let the usher, and the other side, know which room that you are in.

If it is possible to sit *next* to the witness, this is preferable to sitting *opposite* one another. The latter can appear *adversarial*, as though you are interviewing them. Sitting next to a witness, however, so that you can *both* look at a document, is often perceived as *collaborative*, thereby assisting to put a witness at ease. A cup of water can also help.

iii. Break the ice

Before launching into who sits where, speaks first, and how to address the judge, break the ice. Court can be stressful. The journey to court may have been expensive, convoluted, and exhausting. This may be analogous, in a claim following a road traffic collision, to the journey giving rise to the claim.

On other occasions, asking how the journey to court has been can spark a conversation. Whatever the topic, some small talk is preferable to launching into questions about the evidence. Once the ice is broken, and a level of trust and confidence has been established, you can progress to outline the procedure.

iv. Note

It can be worth briefly explaining that you will be taking a note for three reasons.

First, so that, if your *lay* client has any questions about what was said, there is a contemporaneous note. Secondly, so that your *professional* client can see what was discussed. Thirdly, so as to advise on prospects of appealing.

State that the note is *confidential*. It will *not* be shown to the other party, or to the court. It is *solely* for the benefit of the party that you represent. If you wish, you can mark that it is subject to 'legal professional privilege'.

b. Outline the procedure

It can be reassuring to hear how the conference, and then the hearing, is likely to unfold.

i. Before

You are holding a conference, during which you will explain the *procedure* that the court is likely to adopt; ask *questions* so that you understand your lay client's version of events, and fill in any gaps in your instructions; so that you can *advise* on prospects, and *represent* your client's best interests during the hearing.

ii. During

Imagine that you have not been to court before. Who sits where? Who speaks first? How do you address the judge? Witnesses may be comforted by a *brief* overview.

1. Entering & exiting court

Wait for the usher to announce the case. It is etiquette to bow when entering and exiting the courtroom. The bow is more than merely a nod, but less than a full bow, as the torso is not usually parallel to the floor.

If the judge greets the parties, respond appropriately. It is unusual to speak to the judge first. For example, if the judge greets the parties with "good morning", an appropriate response is often to repeat that greeting.

As a rule of thumb, the *claimant* usually sits on the *left*, and the *defendant* sits on the *right*, as one faces the judge.

2. Giving evidence

When giving oral evidence, the following five pieces of guidance may assist.

First, speak *clearly*, *loudly*, and *slowly*. The judge, and both (legal representatives for the) parties will be taking a *note*. Secondly, *answer* the question. If the question misses an important detail, answer the question, *then* add that important detail.

Thirdly, if possible, answer "yes" or "no". A *short* answer is usually more persuasive than a long-winded one. Fourthly, if the question is not understood, ask for it to be repeated. If it is still not understood, ask for it to be put in other words.

Fifthly, it is *not* a memory test. If a relevant date is in your statement, for example, you can look at it. If you cannot remember the answer to a question, just say so.

3. Submissions & judgment

The (advocate for the) claimant does not usually open a case, unless requested to do so by the judge. Claims that are allocated to the small claims track are usually straightforward. There are not often complex issues, of law or fact, necessitating a formal opening.

The court will often be assisted by the claimant opening a final hearing by listing the *issues that are in dispute*, however, *who* is in the courtroom, and which *witnesses (if any)* are needed to give evidence.

In closing, the salient parts of the evidence that assist, or that undermine the competing cases may briefly be summarised, by both parties, so that they are fresh in the mind of the judge, before judgment is given.

iii. After

After the hearing, you will have a brief conference with your *lay* client, so as to explain the result, and outline any next steps. You will also speak to your *professional* client, so as to relay the same, before emailing your attendance note to your *professional* client.

c. Questioning

Collect all of the evidence *on the issues in dispute*. Fill in gaps and clarify any *material* ambiguities in the evidence. Having done so, you should be in a position to provide summary advice on prospects of success, and to go on and represent your client's best interests.

i. Ethics

When questioning, be careful to not lead, or otherwise to suggest, answers to questions that are *in* dispute. This includes verbal, *and* it includes non-verbal communication.

Confirming, and filling in gaps in your instructions, are *different skills* to cross-examination. You are not determining fault, or otherwise giving judgment. You are *advising on what the court is likely to find* on the available evidence.

ii. Active listening

Often, people feel more comfortable relaying *their* version of events, in the way that *they* wish to do so. Then, *once they are happy that they have been understood*, they are usually also comfortable to answer questions.

Often, the quicker you build rapport, using open body language, and active listening skills, the quicker you are able to progress to *effectively and time-efficiently* collecting full instructions.

iii. English

If the witness statement is in English, the witness *must* be able to understand *written* and *spoken* English, unless there is an interpreter.

This means that the witness *must* be able to answer questions in English under *cross*-examination. If it becomes apparent that the witness is unable to do so, or you are otherwise not able to take full instructions in conference, call your professional client *promptly*.

Check whether an interpreter has been booked. If not, was there any indication that an interpreter was needed in the directions questionnaire? If not, and you have to make an application to adjourn, it will be difficult.

There are four reasons, however, why it is preferable to confirm the position *before* the hearing.

First, you can explain the need for an adjournment to the other party, so as to give them an opportunity to make a *joint* submission to the judge that the matter ought to be adjourned. Secondly, an application to adjourn is more likely to succeed if it is *voluntarily* made *before* a hearing, so that you are on the front foot, as opposed to being *forced* to make an application *during* a hearing, when it is clear that a witness cannot understand English to a sufficient level.

Thirdly, as there is a real risk that that witness' evidence will be struck out, and the party that you represent will be unsuccessful, it is preferable to put your *professional* client on *notice* of the same. Fourthly, if you are unable to take instructions in conference, this will become clear in the hearing, and you might, *rightly*, be reprimanded by the court.

iv. Confirm written evidence

A witness should have an opportunity to read a clean, unmarked copy of her statement.

When she has done so, invite a response as to whether or not there is anything to be amended. If there is, take a *word-for-word* note as to which *paragraph* is to be amended, and what *words* are to be substituted. Repeat this back to the witness to confirm that your note is accurate.

If there is no request to amend, enquire whether the statement is accurate. If so, it can be helpful to make a note of it in your attendance note. This is so that, if, under cross-examination, the witness agrees that their statement is *not* accurate, you have a record of having undertaken the above exercise.

Remember to ask *open* questions on issues that are likely to be in dispute. Even if the witness is giving evidence against the case theory of the party who has called her, or the bulk of the evidence, remember your ethical duty *not* to *coach*, or otherwise to *train*, a witness.

Routine witness *preparation*, however, is acceptable.

v. Fill in any gaps

If there is a head of loss that is not evidenced in a party's statement, or otherwise evidenced in the documentation that has been filed and served, ask *open* questions to find out about it.

It may be that, for example, where 'miscellaneous expenses' are claimed, but they are not evidenced, there are receipts, evidencing the same, that that party has brought to the hearing.

Or, the witness may be able to state *what* those expenses were, *when* they were incurred, and *why* they were necessary. If so – and, if permitted by the judge – you could ask a couple of open questions before they are cross-examined, so that this evidence is before the court.

vi. Loss of earnings & expenses

Loss of earnings and expenses can be claimed, should the party for whom a witness gives evidence succeed (see chapter 23(d)(i) and (ii)). These should be noted, so that, ideally, they can be agreed with the other party *before* the hearing; but, *even* if they can*not* be agreed, you will be able swiftly to relay these lost earnings and expenses at the appropriate time (see chapter 15)(g)(v)).

d. Advising

If required to advise, you should now be in a position to do so. If an issue is not properly arguable, then, this should be stated, and the reason for this should be briefly explained.

Counsel must not let their professional discretion be fettered.

Of course, there is a *qualitative* distinction between a point that is not *properly arguable*, and one that is *merely weak*. The former is a *legal* question, *binary*, and involves *professional* ethics. The latter is often grounded in the facts, as the law in a claim that has been allocated to the small claims track is usually well-established.

e. Time management

Usually, you will have up to half an hour for a conference if you have one witness. Where there are multiple witnesses, you will have to manage your time carefully, so as to ensure that you have full instructions before the hearing.

17. Applications

The court may act on the application of a party, or under the court's general powers of case management (CPR 3). In general, applications should be made by issuing an application notice (in accordance with CPR 23). That is, Form N244.

Application for summary judgment, or other early termination, should be made *before*, or *when* filing directions questionnaires (PD 26 at [5.3(1)]). In any event, it should be made as soon as it becomes *apparent* that it is *necessary* or *desirable* (PD 23A at [2.7]).

If it becomes apparent to *you* that an application should be made on the day of the hearing, speak to your professional client, and get *written* instructions via email, to the effect that: your professional client *undertakes* to pay the application *fee*; *issue* the application; and *serve* the application *promptly*, and, in any event, within *three* working days.

Then, you can invite the court to exercise its general powers of case management, but, failing that, you can make an application on instructions. *Counsel* should *never* undertake to file and serve an application, or to pay a fee; *professional clients* give undertakings.

a. Default judgment

"Default judgment" means judgment without a hearing, where there has been no acknowledgment of service, or defence. Where a defendant in a claim, or a claimant in a counterclaim, fails to file and serve a defence, default judgment may be entered.

It is in accordance with the overriding objective to deal with an *un*defended claim (or counterclaim), *justly*, as it is *un*defended, and at *proportionate cost*, as there is no need for directions or a final hearing.

i. Administrative

A party merely has to file a *request* for judgment to be entered. *Administrative* staff (as opposed to a judge) can enter judgment. There is *no* consideration of the *merits* of the claim.

ii. Excluded claims

There are five types of claim that may be allocated to the small claims track in which default judgment cannot be entered.

First, claims for the delivery of goods, subject to an agreement regulated by the Consumer Credit Act 1974 (CPR 12.2(a)). Secondly, Part 8 claims (CPR 12.2(b)). Thirdly, where the defendant has applied for strike out, or summary judgment, and that application has not been disposed of (CPR 12.3(3)(a)).

Fourthly, where the defendant has satisfied the whole claim, including any claim for costs, on which the claimant is seeking judgment (CPR 12.3(3)(b)). Fifthly, the claimant is seeking judgment on a claim for money, and the defendant has filed, or has served an admission of liability to pay all of the money, together with a request for time to pay (CPR 12.3(3)(c)).

iii. Default of acknowledgement of service

When two conditions are met, claimants may obtain default judgment in default of an acknowledgment of service (CPR 12.3(1)). First, the defendant has not filed an acknowledgment of service or defence. Secondly, the relevant time period for doing the same has expired.

iv. Default of defence

Where two conditions are met, claimants may obtain default judgment in default of a defence (CPR 12.3(2)). First, *acknowledgment of service* has been filed, but *not* a *defence*; and, in a *counter*claim, a *defence* to that *counter*claim has *not* been filed. Secondly, the relevant time limit for doing the same has expired.

v. Procedure

In general, claimants can obtain default judgment by filling in a request in the relevant form where the claim is for any of the following (CPR 12.4(1)).

First, a specified amount of money. Secondly, an amount of money to be decided by the court. Thirdly, delivery of goods, where the claim form gives the defendant the alternative of paying their value. Fourthly, any combination of these remedies.

There are separate forms for specified, *un*specified, and *non*-money claims.

vi. Set aside

Where default judgment was wrongly entered, it *must* be set aside (CPR 13.2).

Where the defendant has a *real prospect of successfully defending* the claim, or it appears that there is *some other good reason* why the defendant should be allowed to defend the claim, the court *may* (that is, has a *discretion* to) set aside default judgment (CPR 13.3).

Where there is a discretion, the court will take into account whether or not the party seeking to set aside made the application promptly (CPR 13.3(2)). That application must be supported by evidence (CPR 13.4(3)).

These powers may be exercised on application of a party, or on the court's own motion.

b. Transfer

Application can be made to the court in which the case is being heard for that case to be transferred to another court. If so, there should be a *good* reason.

For example, distance to the court, disability, or childcare commitments. These should have been set out in the directions questionnaire, however, *before* the case was transferred.

c. Consent

Where the parties agree an order, or agree a judgment, that may be entered, and sealed (CPR 40.6).

Where the parties have written to the court, consenting to the making of an order that has been filed in draft form, they must ensure that they provide the court with any material that is needed to satisfy the court that it is appropriate to make the order. In general, a *letter* will be acceptable.

The draft order must be in the terms that have been agreed, expressed to be 'by consent', and it must be signed by the (legal representatives of the) parties (CPR 40.6(7)). Where a hearing date has been fixed, the parties must inform the court immediately (PD 23A at [10.5]).

d. Summary judgment

Summary judgment is closely related to the jurisdiction to strike out (CPR 3.4 and PD 3A at [1.7]). It gives a wider scope, however, for dismissing a claim, or a defence (*Monsanto Plc v Tilly* [2000] Env LR 313 at [19]).

It is a procedure by which the court may decide a claim, or a particular issue, *without* a final hearing (CPR 24.1). A party may apply for summary judgment (PD 26 at [5.2]).

i. When

The application should normally be made between the acknowledgment of service, and the filing of the applicant's directions questionnaire (PD 26 at [5.3(1)]).

Where an application is made, the court will not normally allocate the claim before hearing the application. Where a party files a directions questionnaire, stating that she *intends* to make such an application, but has *not* yet done so, the court will usually direct that an allocation hearing is listed.

ii. Allocation hearing

The application may be heard at the allocation hearing, if the application notice has been issued, and it has been served in sufficient time. If summary judgment is granted before allocation, the general rule is that the successful party can apply for costs, which are *not* limited to those otherwise available on the small claims track (CPRs 46.11(2) and 46.13(3)).

iii. Grounds

There are two grounds (CPR 24.2).

First, no real prospect of succeeding on the claim, defence, or issue. This means that it must carry some *degree of conviction*, as opposed to being *merely fanciful*, and more than *merely* arguable. The standard is therefore *not* on a balance of probabilities.

Secondly, there is no other *compelling* reason why the case, or issue, should be disposed of at a final hearing.

The *burden* of proof is on the *applicant*.

e. Strike out

Strike out is closely related to the jurisdiction to enter summary judgment (CPR 24 and PD 3A at [1.7]).

In general, where properly arguable, an application should apply for *both*, however, the court *may* treat an application for *strike out* as one for *summary judgment*, so as to dispose of issues, claims, or defences, that do not deserve full investigation, and a final hearing (*Three Rivers District Council & Ors v Governor & Company of the Bank of England (No 3)* [2001] UKHL 16, [2003] 2 AC 1 at [88]).

i. When

If an application is not made before directions questionnaires must be filed, the intention to make an application should be included in the directions questionnaire (PD 26 at [2.2(3)(a)]).

Where a statement of case is not verified by a statement of truth, a party may apply to the court for an order that, *unless* it is verified by the service of a statement of truth, within such *period* as the court may specify, it will *automatically* be struck out (PD 22 at [4.2]).

ii. Grounds

The court may strike out (any part of) a statement of case if one (or more) of the following three conditions are satisfied (CPR 3.4(2)).

First, it discloses *no reasonable grounds* for bringing or defending the claim. Secondly, it is an *abuse* of the court's process, or otherwise *likely to obstruct the just disposal* of proceedings. Thirdly, there has been a *failure to comply* with a rule, practice direction, or court order.

The court also has *separate* power to strike out a statement of case that is *not* verified by a *statement of truth* (CPR 22.2(2)).

1. No reasonable grounds

Where a statement of case does *not* set out a *clear* statement of facts, it is *in*coherent, or, *even* if correct, it does *not* amount to a cause of action, or a defence that is *recognised in law*, it discloses no reasonable grounds.

In such a case, the offending statement of case may be amended, upon application, with permission of the court, exercising its discretion, in accordance with the overriding objective.

2. Abuse of process & obstructing just disposal

In *Hunter v Chief Constable of the West Midlands Police & Ors* [1981] UKHL 13, [1982] AC 529 ("*Hunter*") at 526, Lord Diplock defined an "abuse of process" in these terms (with emphasis added):

> "It concerns the inherent power which any court of justice must possess to prevent misuse of its procedure in a way which, although not inconsistent with the literal application of its procedural rules, would nevertheless be *manifestly unfair to a party* to litigation before it, or would *otherwise bring the administration of justice into disrepute* among right-thinking people. The circumstances in which abuse of process can arise are very varied; …"

In cases that are allocated to the small claims track, the most common forms of abuse are likely to include the following.

First, a *collateral* attack on a factual issue *decided* in another *court* of competent jurisdiction (*Hunter*). Secondly, *res judicata*. That is, where there has already been a *final* decision, on the *same* cause of action, between the *same* parties, in which the issue in dispute in the earlier, decided claim, and the latter, undecided claim, are *identical*.

Thirdly, where a later claim *could*, and *should* have been made in *previous* proceedings (*Henderson v Henderson* [1843-60] All ER Rep 378 at 381). Fourthly, where the claim has already been settled, or otherwise compromised. For example, through a binding settlement agreement.

3. Default

The most frequent examples in cases that are allocated to the small claims track are where there is no *statement of truth*, failure to comply with an *unless* order, or where a party who is *unable to read or to sign* a statement of truth, nonetheless purports to do so.

a. Statement of truth

If a statement of case is *not* verified by a statement of truth, it *remains* effective, *unless* it is struck out. A party may *not* rely on the contents of a statement of case as *evidence*, however, *until* it has been *verified* by a statement of truth (PD 22 at [4.1]).

b. Unless order

Failure to comply with an unless order, for example, to fully particularise the allegations in the particulars of claim, within such period as the court may specify, will mean that the statement of case is *automatically* struck out (CPR 3.8(1)).

c. Inability to read or sign

Where a document containing a statement of truth is to be signed by a person who is unable to read, or to sign, that document must contain a certificate made by an authorised person (PD 22 at [3A.1]).

An authorised person is a person able to administer oaths, and take affidavits, but need not be independent of the parties, or independent of their representatives. She must certify five requirements (PD 22 at [3A.3]).

First, the document has been *read* to the person who is signing it. Secondly, that person appeared to *understand* it, and *approved* its content as *accurate*. Thirdly, the *declaration of truth* has been *read* to that person.

Fourthly, that person appeared to *understand* the *declaration*, and the *consequences* of making a *false* declaration. Fifthly, that person *signed*, or made her *mark*, in the *presence* of the *authorised* person.

The form of certificate is prescribed (PD 22 at appendix 1):

> I certify that I [*name and address of authorised person*] have read over the contents of this document and the declaration of truth to the person signing the document [*if there are exhibits, add and explain the nature and effect of the exhibits referred to in it*] who appeared to understand (a) the document and approved its content as accurate and (b) the declaration of truth and the consequences of making a false declaration, and made his mark in my presence.

f. Adjourn

Contact the other side to find out whether or not an adjournment can be *agreed by consent*, subject to the court making the order.

If not, an *application* will have to be made, and a *good* reason will have to be given, evidencing the need to adjourn, *contrary* to the wishes of the other party.

Under the court's general case-management powers, the court may adjourn a hearing (CPR 3.1(2)(b) and PD 27 at [6.2]). When deciding whether or not to adjourn a hearing, as with all other exercises of the court's discretion, the court must further the *overriding objective*.

i. Overriding objective

The overriding objective to deal with a case justly and proportionately, so far as practicable, includes the following four considerations (CPR 1.1(2)).

First, saving expense. Secondly, dealing with the case in a way which is proportionate to the: amount of money involved; importance of the case; and financial position of each party. Thirdly, ensuring that the case is dealt with expeditiously and fairly.

Fourthly, allotting an appropriate share of the court's resources to the case, while taking into account the need to allot resources to other cases. These are likely to form the bones of an application to adjourn.

ii. Health

Where a witness cannot attend, but the evidence that she would be able to give would make no *material* difference to the *outcome* of the case, the court should *refuse* to adjourn.

Where a litigant in person shows *real* grounds that her alleged ill-health is *genuine*, however, the court will usually allow an adjournment. To establish real grounds, medical evidence may be expected, which the court should scrutinise carefully. In an ideal situation, this will satisfy the following four criteria (*General Medical Council v Hayat* [2018] EWCA Civ 2796 at [38]).

First, the *medical professional* should be *identified*. Secondly, she should give details as to her *familiarity* with the party's *medical condition*, detailing *recent* consultations.

Thirdly, the party's medical condition should be *identified*, with the *features* of that condition, which, in the medical professional's opinion, *prevent* that party attending the final hearing. Fourthly, there should be a *reasoned prognosis* (that is, likely course of the medical condition).

The court is *not* bound to accept medical (or any other expert) evidence. If the court rejects medical evidence, however, there should be a good reason for doing so.

Notwithstanding the above, if a party, or other witness is *needed for the case to be dealt with justly*, but she is unable to be present, *through no fault of her own*, the court will usually grant an adjournment, however disproportionate it may appear.

One example is where a party has been admitted to an accident and emergency department of a hospital.

If the court has reservations, it may give directions so as to resolve any doubts. For example, that (further) medical evidence be filed and served promptly. If good evidence is not later provided, there may be costs consequences.

g. Set aside

A party may apply for an order that judgment is set aside, and that the claim is reheard, provided that two conditions are satisfied (CPR 27.11(1)).

First, she was neither present, nor represented, at the hearing. Secondly, she did not give written notice to the court, requesting that the claim be decided in her absence.

The application must be made not more than 14 days after the day on which notice of the judgment was served on her. The court may only grant the application if two conditions are satisfied (CPR 27.11(3)).

First, the applicant had a *good* reason for not attending, being represented at the hearing, or giving written notice to the court. Secondly, she has a *reasonable prospect of success*.

An application can*not* be made where the parties agreed to deal with the claim without a hearing (CPR 27.11(5)).

If the application is successful, the court must fix a new date for hearing the claim, which may take place *immediately* after the application to set aside. It may also be dealt with by the *same* judge who set aside judgment (CPR 27.11(4)).

h. Relief from sanctions

Where there has been a failure to comply with a rule, practice direction, or court order, any sanction has effect, unless the party in default applies for, and in fact obtains, relief from sanctions (CPR 3.8).

i. Need

Before making a formal application for relief from sanctions, check whether the rule, practice direction, or court order, in fact *specifies* a *sanction*.

If not, and there is *no* automatic sanction, then there is *no* need to apply for relief from sanctions, as *no* sanction has taken effect.

Standard directions in a case that has been allocated to the small claims track usually include that the judge 'may refuse to hear' evidence that has not been prepared, filed, and served, in accordance with the directions in the notice of allocation.

There is a *material* difference between *may refuse to hear*, and, for example, failure to comply with an *unless* order. The former provides the court with a *discretion* as to whether to *impose* a sanction. An unless order, however, *specifies a sanction*, such as, 'shall stand automatically struck out'.

The latter therefore requires an application to grant relief from a sanction *that has taken effect*. This is an important distinction. When exercising any discretion, the court should seek to further the overriding objective. Accordingly, *all* of the factors that are encompassed within the overriding objective may be deployed in submissions *against imposing a sanction*.

ii. Evidence

An application must be supported by evidence (CPR 3.9(2)).

It should be made in accordance with Part 23, and there should usually be a witness statement in support, frequently written, and signed, by a professional client. If the breach arises unexpectedly on the day of the hearing, an *oral* application may be necessary.

iii. Three-stage test

The court will apply the following three-stage test when deciding whether or not to grant relief from sanctions (*Denton & Ors v TH White Ltd & Ors* [2014] EWCA Civ 906, [2015] 1 All ER 880 ("*Denton*") at [24]):

> "… The first stage is to identify and assess the seriousness and significance of the 'failure to comply with any rule, practice direction or court order' which engages rule 3.9(1). If the breach is neither serious nor significant, the court is unlikely to need to spend much time on the second and third stages. The second stage is to consider why the default occurred. The third stage is to evaluate 'all the circumstances of the case, so as to enable [the court] to deal justly with the application including [factors (a) and (b)]'. …"

1. Seriousness & significance

Stage one is not concerned with previous breaches ("*Denton*" at [27]):

"The assessment of the seriousness or significance of the breach should not, initially at least, involve a consideration of other unrelated failures that may have occurred in the past. At the first stage, the court should concentrate on an assessment of the seriousness and significance of the very breach in respect of which relief from sanctions is sought. ..."

If this breach is not serious, or significant, the court *should* usually grant relief.

2. Reason

Stage two is not whether there is *a* reason. There will always be *a* reason.

It is testing whether or not there is a *good* reason.

The Court of Appeal consider that "good reasons are likely to arise from circumstances outside the control of the party in default" (*Andrew Mitchell MP v News Group Newspapers Ltd* [2013] EWCA Civ 1537, [2014] 2 All ER 430 ("*Mitchell*") at [43] and *Denton* at [30]).

Failure caused solely by a legal representative will *rarely* amount to a *good* reason (*Mitchell* at [41] and *Denton* at [12]):

"...Solicitors cannot take on too much work and expect to be able to persuade a court that this is a good reason for their failure to meet deadlines. They should either delegate the work to others in their firm or, if they are unable to do this, they should not take on the work at all. ..."

Failure to *consult*, lack of *authority*, and *evidence* of the same, are usually *necessary* to *even begin* to argue that failure of a legal representative amounts to a good reason (*Training in Compliance Ltd (t/a Matthew Reed) v Dewse (t/a Data Research Co)* [2001] CP Rep 46 at [66]):

"… Of course, if there is evidence put before the court that a party was not consulted and did not give his consent to what the legal representatives had done in his name, the court may have regard to that as a fact, though it does not follow that it would necessarily, or even probably, lead to a limited order against the legal representatives. It seems to me that, in general, the action or inaction of a party's legal representatives must be treated under the Civil Procedure Rules as the action or inaction of the party himself."

3. All the circumstances

An application following a serious, significant breach, for which there is no good reason, is, however, *not* doomed to fail.

Where submissions on the first two stages are not properly arguable, concede them. You will gain *credibility* with the court, and you will be able to invest *more* time in the third stage of the test, which is *virtually* always properly arguable.

When deciding whether or not to grant relief from sanctions, the court will have regard to *all* the circumstances of the case, but two, *in particular*, are *paramount* (CPR 3.9(1)).

First, that litigation is conducted *efficiently*, and at *proportionate cost*. Secondly, to *enforce compliance* with rules, practice directions, and court orders. These two circumstances are "of particular importance and should be given particular weight" (*Denton* at [35]).

a. Proportionality

The court will consider whether the *sanction* is *proportionate* to the *breach*. Where the defendant would be left with no evidence, the claim is for just shy of £10,000, and the defendant has a fully particularised, properly arguable defence, for example, proportionality may be a strong factor in favour of granting relief.

b. Compliance

The court "must always bear in mind the need for compliance … because the old lax culture of non-compliance is no longer tolerated" (*Denton* at [34]).

If there are multiple breaches, this can be an especially potent circumstance because this is the stage of the test where previous breaches may also be taken into account.

c. Promptness

This circumstance is capable of being *decisive*.

If an application for relief is made *promptly*, the other party may be under an *obligation* to consent to that application, so as to discourage *opportunism*. On the other hand, it may be the "critical factor" where the delay has "substantially disrupted the progress of the action" (*Oak Cash & Carry Ltd v British Gas Trading Ltd* [2016] EWCA Civ 153, [2016] 4 All ER 129 at [61]).

d. Opportunism

It is a *breach* of the *duty of the parties* to help the court to further the *overriding objective* to resist *opportunistically* an application for relief that is *bound* to succeed (*Denton* at [43]):

> "… It is as unacceptable for a party to try to take advantage of a minor inadvertent error, as it is for rules, orders and practice directions to be breached in the first place. Heavy costs sanctions should, therefore, be imposed on parties who behave unreasonably in refusing to agree extensions of time or unreasonably oppose applications for relief from sanctions. …"

Where an application for relief from sanctions is unreasonably opposed, this should form (at least) one basis of a submission that the *manner* in which the opposing party has conducted her case shows that she has behaved unreasonably (see chapter 24(c)(iv)(7)). Accordingly, she should pay the costs of *resisting* the application.

18. Procedure of the final hearing

This chapter covers the *procedure* that the final hearing is likely to adopt.

It includes: the *judge*; *representation*; the general rule that hearings are *recorded* in *public*; evidence is *not* usually on oath; cross-examination may be *limited*; and the line between judicial intervention and "entering the arena".

a. Judge

All of the judicial functions under the procedure for dealing with claims that are allocated to the small claims track will generally be carried out by a (deputy) district judge.

In principle, they *may* be carried out by a *circuit* judge (PD 27 at [1]), provided that she *consents* (PD 2B at [11.2(1)]). In practice, this is very rare. Appeal from a circuit judge is to a High Court judge.

b. Representation

A party may be represented by a lawyer. In practice, usually counsel, or solicitor.

They may also be represented by a lay representative, provided that that party is present throughout the hearing (PD 27 at [3.2]).

Further to article 3 of the Lay Representatives (Right of Audience) Order 1999 (SI 1999/1225), the court's permission is required where a party wishes to be represented by a lay representative in three circumstances (PD 27 at [3.2(2)]).

First, her client does not attend the hearing. Secondly, at any stage after judgment. Thirdly, on any appeal brought against any decision made by a district judge.

Section 11 of the Courts and Legal Services Act 1990 prescribes that, where the court is of the opinion that a person, who would otherwise have a right of audience, is behaving in an *unruly* manner in any proceedings, the court may *refuse* to hear that person in *those* proceedings. If so, the court must *specify* the conduct that warranted refusal.

Where the court has reason to believe that a person *intentionally* has misled the court, or otherwise demonstrates that she is *un*suitable to exercise a right of audience, in the instant, or any other, proceedings, the court may order that person's *disqualification* from exercising any *right of audience* in proceedings in the county court. Again, the court *must* give reasons.

Appeal lies to the Court of Appeal. Any such order may be revoked, however, at any time, by any county court judge.

Any of a corporate party's officers, or employees, may represent that party (PD 27 at [3.2(4)]).

c. Public

Claims that are allocated to the small claims track *must* be heard in *public*. If there is any doubt as to whether or not it is a well-established, *common law* right, it is certainly a well-established, *statutory* right. This is pursuant to article 6 of the European Convention on Human Rights, which a court, as a public authority, must act compatibly with, pursuant to section 6 of the Human Rights Act 1998.

d. Recording

Recording may be *official*, in accordance with the rules and practice directions of court. Or, it may be *un*official, so that it is in *contempt* of court.

i. Official

Hearings *will* be tape recorded (PD 27 at [5.1]).

On payment of the relevant fee to the transcriber, *a party* may obtain a transcript of this recording. The position is different where a person is *not* a party.

In any event, *Practice Direction (Audio Recordings of Proceedings: Access)* [2014] 1 WLR 632 means that "there is generally no right for either a party or a non-party to listen to the recording" (*Cape Intermediate Holdings Ltd v Dring (Asbestos Victims Support Groups Forum UK)* [2019] UKSC 38, [2019] 3 WLR 429 at [25]).

ii. Unofficial

Attention is drawn to section 9 of the Contempt of Court Act 1981, and *Practice Direction (Tape Recorders)* [1981] 1 WLR 1526, which relate to *un*official recordings (PD 27 at [5.2]).

1. Contempt of Court Act 1981

Section 9(1) of the Contempt of Court Act 1981 concerns the *un*authorised use of tape recorders in court. It provides, so far as is relevant:

> … it is a contempt of court—
>
> (a) to use in court, or bring into court for use, any tape recorder or other instrument for recording sound, except with the leave of the court;

(b) to publish a recording of legal proceedings made by means of any such instrument, or any recording derived directly or indirectly from it, by playing it in the hearing of the public or any section of the public, or to dispose of it or any recording so derived, with a view to such publication;

(c) to use any such recording in contravention of any conditions of leave granted under paragraph (a).

2. Practice Direction (Tape Recorders) [1981] 1 WLR 1526

Practice Direction (Tape Recorders) [1981] 1 WLR 1526 provides guidance as to the *discretion* of the court to grant, withhold, or withdraw, leave to use tape recorders, or to impose *conditions* as to the use of the recording. This discretion is *un*limited.

The then Lord Chief Justice identified that the following three factors *may* be relevant.

First, any reasonable *need* for the recording. Whether a litigant, a person connected with the press, or broadcasting. Secondly, the risk that the recording would be used to brief witnesses out of court, where a direction has been made to exclude one or more witnesses from court. Thirdly, the possibility that proceedings will be *disturbed*, witnesses, or other participants, would be *distracted*, or otherwise *worried*.

Consideration should be given to whether or not *conditions* should be imposed. The *identity* of the person applying to use a tape recorder, and her role in the proceedings, may be relevant. Where permission is given, it is *not* intended to be used as, or compete with, the official transcript.

3. Sentence

An 87-year-old man was sentenced to 28 days' imprisonment for each contempt of court, namely, making video or audio recordings of proceedings, and publishing them on the internet. Although *not* an *immediate* custodial sentence, it was nevertheless a custodial sentence, albeit suspended for 12 months (*Attorney General v Scarth* [2013] EWHC 194 (Admin)).

e. Evidence

The court need *not* take evidence on oath (CPR 27.8(4)).

In practice, evidence is not on oath. One reason is that cases involving a disputed allegation of dishonesty will *not* usually be *suitable* for, and, therefore, will *not* usually be *allocated* to, the small claims track (PD 26 at [8.1(1)(d)]).

f. Cross-examination

The court may adopt *any* method of *proceeding* that the court considers to be *fair* (CPR 27.8(1)). In particular, this includes the following four powers (PD 27 at [4.3]).

First, to ask questions of any witness, before allowing any other person to do so. Secondly, to ask questions of all, or any of the witnesses, before allowing any other person to ask questions of any witnesses.

Thirdly, to refuse to allow cross-examination of any witness, until all the witnesses have given evidence in chief. Fourthly, to limit cross-examination of a witness to a fixed time frame, or to a particular subject, issue, or both.

The court cannot, however, prevent *any* cross-examination. As per *Al Rawi & Ors v The Security Service & Ors* [2011] UKSC 34, [2012] 1 AC 531:

"10. There are certain features of a common law trial which are fundamental to our system of justice (both criminal and civil). ...

11. The open justice principle is not a mere procedural rule. It is a fundamental common law principle. ...

13. Another aspect of the principle of natural justice is that the parties should be given the opportunity to call their own witnesses and to cross-examine the opposing witnesses. ..."

g. Judicial intervention v entering the arena

There is a distinction between *judicial intervention*, which is sanctioned by the CPR, and "entering the arena", which is *not*.

Authority provides guidance as to how far judges may go before a party has a legitimate grievance that the overriding objective has not been achieved because the parties were not on an equal footing.

i. Judicial intervention

The court may ask questions of any witness herself, before allowing any other person to do so, and ask questions of all, or any of the witnesses herself, before allowing any other person to ask questions of any witnesses (PD 27 at [4.3]).

When contrasted to claims that have been allocated to the fast track, or to the multi-track, this can appear much more *inquisitorial* (as opposed to *adversarial*). Although this can be the case, judges should be cautious *not* to enter the arena.

Especially when *both* parties are legally *represented*.

ii. Entering the arena

The leading case is *Serafin v Malkiewicz & Ors* [2019] EWCA Civ 852, [2019] EMLR 21 ("*Serafin*"). Lewison, McCombe and Haddon-Cave LJJ set out the law under the heading: 'The principle of fairness'.

1. Fairness

It is the *duty* of a judge to *intervene*, so as to ask questions that *clarify ambiguities* in answers previously given, or, for example, that *identify the nature* of the defence, if this is unclear.

At paragraph 110 of *Serafin*, the court said that it is *wrong*, however, for a judge to "descend into the arena and give the impression of acting as advocate".

Whether a hearing has been *fair* is *not* to be judged *just* by the correctness of the result. Not all departures from good practice render a hearing unfair. The question is one of degree, however, there is *no* special rule for litigants in person. At paragraph 112, the court continued:

> "These principles, of course, apply with equal rigour whether or not litigants are legally represented. Indeed, so far as litigants in person are concerned, judges and tribunals should be (and generally are) especially conscious to ensure the dictates of fairness are observed – and seen to be observed – at all times and that due allowance is always made for language and other difficulties."

Where any of the following circumstances can be identified, depending on the *degree*, *nature*, *tenor*, and *frequency*, of intervention, a judge may have entered the arena.

First, cross-examination. Secondly, use of bullying, threatening, or overbearing language. Thirdly, given the impression of hostility, animosity, or ill feeling towards a party.

Where the relevant party is *un*represented, or English is *not* her first language, these facts are likely to push an appeal court towards a finding of *manifest* unfairness.

In *Karen Shaw v Peter David Grouby & Anor* [2017] EWCA Civ 233 ("*Shaw*") at [45], Lord Justice Pattern said that:

> "I have to say at the outset that the judge's interventions, whilst always courteous, were in my opinion excessive and that he should have attempted to postpone his questioning, particularly of the witnesses of fact, until after counsel had conducted his cross-examination except when it was necessary to ask the witness to clarify an answer so that the judge could understand the evidence that was being given. …"

The test for an appeal court is whether the judge became *so* involved in the *examination* of *witnesses* that it was *im*possible for *counsel* to conduct her client's case, or lost the ability to reach *balanced, objective* conclusions on the *evidence*.

To use the words of the Chancellor of the High Court in *Shaw* at paragraph 65, "continuous interruptions during cross-examination can so often do more harm than good."

2. Guidance

Serafin and *Shaw* were not allocated to the small claims track, however, they provide useful, *practical* principles on fairness for *any* common law, *adversarial* final hearing. There are seven further useful pieces of guidance.

First, keep your cool. If there is a sense (on the transcript of proceedings) that you are discourteous, argumentative, or otherwise dramatising, it will make any appeal more difficult. Secondly, do not make an application for recusal, unless the unfairness is *absolutely* clear. Thirdly, if it is clear, do not wait till the end of the hearing. Make the application promptly.

Fourthly, if you know of the reason for the *real*, or (more likely) *potential* partiality, you may be held to have waived any right to raise it if you do not say something early on. For example, personal friendship, or animosity between the judge and any member of the public involved in the case, both constitute "a real danger of bias" (*Locabail (UK) Ltd v Bayfield Properties Ltd & Anor* [1999] EWCA Civ 3004, [2000] QB 451 at [25]).

Fifthly, if you identify any obvious unfairness, find a courteous, professional way to convey your concern. In *Serafin* at paragraph 116, it is noted that counsel said (with emphasis added):

> "… *I just wanted to give Mr Serafin the opportunity because he's not represented*, and despite my Lord being, if I may say so, very fair in terms of ensuring that he understands everything very carefully …"

To this, the appeal judgment provides that: "(We detect more than a note of concern in the fact that [counsel] felt that he had to make the last observation)."

Sixthly, your professional, ethical duty, requires you to put your client's interest first, not your career. You protect the latter through keeping *calm*, strict adherence to professional *ethics*, and reasoned *judgement*. Seventhly, speak to other members of chambers, who may know the judge, and seek *their* counsel.

19. Witness evidence

Witness evidence includes witness statements, and oral evidence.

It is usually an essential ingredient of a party's case. To the extent the evidence of a witness *chimes* with *agreed* or *known* facts, a judge is likely to follow it when giving judgment. Where it is *in*compatible, however, the credibility of that witness will *diminish*; and so, her ability to give evidence that assists the party who called her, will *decline* correspondingly.

a. Contemporaneous

After a road traffic collision, a witness may complete a *questionnaire*.

Often, on the same day, or shortly thereafter. It is likely to state the *location* of the collision, the *registration* number of the relevant vehicles, and the *mechanism* of the collision.

There may also be a *sketch* plan indicating, for example: the *lane* a vehicle was in; whether the claimant's vehicle was in front or behind the defendant's vehicle; which part of the defendant's vehicle collided with which part of the claimant's vehicle; who was at *fault*; and the *reason* why.

Check whether the questionnaire is signed and dated. Is it contemporaneous to the collision?

If so, it is likely to pre-date a witness statement by many days, months, or even years. In this case, if it is *also* consistent with a witness' written or oral evidence, this can be particularly persuasive, *contemporaneous* evidence.

Even more so if the author of the questionnaire is not a party, but an *independent* witness, who was previously unknown to either party (see chapter 20(a)).

If it is *in*consistent with a witness' *written*, or *oral* evidence, it is likely to be good evidence on which to cross-examine. A concession in cross-examination that there is no good reason why a witness has *changed* her account – be it in the form of a witness statement, or answers to questions in cross-examination – can *undermine* that witness as a *reliable* historian of events.

To use the often-quoted words of Lord Pearce in *Onassis v Vergottis* [1968] 2 Lloyd's Rep 403 at 431: "With every day that passes memory becomes fainter and the imagination becomes more active".

Check whether the document has been disclosed to the other party. If in doubt, speak to your professional client. If it has not, the judge may refuse to admit it.

If you print off copies for the court, the other party, and the witness, however, the other party may agree to its admission. If they do not, then, an oral application can be made to the judge, requesting permission, where it is in accordance with the overriding objective.

b. Statements

A witness statement is a written statement, signed by a person, containing the evidence that that person would be allowed to give orally.

At a final hearing, where a witness is called to give oral evidence, her witness statement will stand as her evidence in chief, unless the court otherwise orders. That witness will usually be cross-examined, often by (the advocate for) the other party.

The witness' answers in *both* examination in *chief* and *cross*-examination constitute that witness' *oral* evidence.

i. Formalities

The rule prescribing the form of a witness statement is *expressly* disapplied in claims that are allocated to the small claims track (CPRs 27.2(1)(c), 32.8, and PD 32).

Although the *strict* rules of evidence do not apply to cases that have been allocated to the small claims track, witness statements should *aspire* to follow the *same* formalities as are necessary in claims that have been allocated to the fast track, or to the multi-track.

ii. Form

A witness statement should have a header, setting out the names of the parties, case number, and court that the matter will be heard in. It should have numbered paragraphs, be in a legible font, and the text should be sized so that it can be read easily.

In any event, where witness statements are relied on, standard directions usually include that they must be filed, served, and comply with the following five criteria.

First, state the case name, and the claim number. Secondly, state the full name, and the full address of the witness. Thirdly, set out the witness' evidence clearly, in numbered paragraphs, on numbered pages. Fourthly, end with: 'I believe that the facts stated in this witness statement are true' (or words to that effect). Fifthly, be signed by the witness and dated.

iii. Statement of truth

The rule requiring witness statements to be verified by a statement of truth (CPR 22.1(1)(c)) is *not* disapplied in claims that are allocated to the small claims track.

Legal representatives are not permitted to sign witness statements on behalf of their clients. A witness statement must be signed by the witness who confirms the truth of it (PD 22 at [3.2]).

The form of a statement of truth is as follows (PD 22 [2.1]): 'I believe that the facts stated in this witness statement are true.'

Where there is no statement of truth, the court may direct that it shall not be admissible as evidence (CPR 22.3).

iv. Inability to read or sign

Where a person is unable to read or sign a statement, it must contain a certificate made by an authorised person (PD 22 at [3A.1]).

An authorised person is a person able to administer oaths, and to take affidavits, but need not be independent of the parties, or independent of their representatives. That person must certify that five requirements have been met.

First, that the document has been *read* to the person signing it. Secondly, that person appeared to *understand* it, and *approved* its content as *accurate*. Thirdly, the *declaration* of truth has been *read* to that person.

Fourthly, that person appeared to *understand* the *declaration*, and the *consequences* of making a *false* declaration. Fifthly, that person *signed*, or made her *mark*, in the *presence* of the *authorised* person.

The form of the certificate is prescribed (in PD 22 at appendix 1):

I certify that I [*name and address of authorised person*] have read over the contents of this document and the declaration of truth to the person signing the document [*if there are exhibits, add* and explain the nature and effect of the exhibits referred to in it"] who appeared to understand (a) the document and approved its content as accurate and (b) the declaration of truth and the consequences of making a false declaration, and made his mark in my presence.

v. Contemporaneous

Look at the date that the statement is *dated*.

In the context of a road traffic collision, for example, it may have been written months, or, in many cases, *years* after the collision. Drawing the court's attention to how *long* after the collision that it was signed can *reduce* the *weight* that the court will attach to it.

The period between the date of the collision, and the date that the statement is signed, can be calculated, so that your submission is precise.

If the statement is dated shortly after the collision, and, in oral evidence, the witness contradicts a key fact that is confirmed to be true within it, the point should be made that their recollection is likely to have been greater when their statement was written, when compared to the (often much) later date that oral evidence is given.

Accordingly, in this circumstance, where *later, oral* evidence is *in*consistent with *earlier, written* evidence, the *latter* will likely be given *more* weight. A submission that that party's case is *internally in*consistent can be made in closing submissions.

vi. Detail

Witness statements should be *detailed*.

This means that in a claim for repairs and credit hire following a road traffic collision, for example, a few paragraphs in the claimant's statement are unlikely to be sufficient to convey the necessary detail that is required to discharge the burden of proof.

There will usually be a detail or two, and sometimes many "important" details which, following cross-examination, it is clear that a witness has omitted from her statement. This is one purpose of cross-examination.

Quality, but also, *quantity* is important.

If a single, but *vital* fact has been omitted, that might be sufficient severely to undermine a witness' credibility. On the other hand, where a number of less important facts are left out of a statement, this is likely to be more understandable, and so less likely to undermine credibility substantially.

In a road traffic collision, the location, and the mechanism of the collision, should both be set out, clearly, and *in detail*.

In a claim for credit hire, the need to hire should be set out in reasonable detail. 'Social, domestic and pleasure' is insufficient. It is legal jargon that people do not use in everyday life, and likely to have been inserted by a legal representative.

'I needed a vehicle to drop off my two, young children to school in the morning, and to take my eldest child to judo on Tuesday and Thursday evenings' is approaching the particularity required.

vii. Hearsay notice

If a witness is unable to attend a hearing, there is no *formal* need for a hearsay notice. Nevertheless, one is often provided by a party that is represented (it being necessary for cases allocated to the fast track, and to the multi-track).

It is also good practice, and courteous, promptly to inform another party of the reason that a witness is no longer able to attend a hearing. There is a legitimate expectation that a witness who has taken the time to produce a statement will attend to give oral evidence.

With*out* having the benefit of being cross-examined, the evidence that a witness is able to give may be given little, if *any*, weight.

Take a claim after a road traffic collision in which liability is in dispute.

It is unlikely that a claimant whose witness failed to attend will be able to discharge the burden of proving that the defendant's driving fell below a reasonable standard. Likewise, a defendant whose witness did not attend will likely be found liable where a claimant gives oral evidence that the defendant's driving caused a collision, due to her lack of care and attention.

viii. Non-attendance

It is worth noting here, again, that the *strict* rules of evidence do *not* apply.

The Civil Evidence Act 1995, however, is a useful starting point. Section 4 prescribes that, when attributing weight to hearsay evidence, the court 'shall have regard to any circumstances from which any inference can reasonably be drawn as to the reliability or otherwise of the evidence'.

1. Factors

This section also provides that the court does not have to attribute *any* weight to hearsay evidence. If it does, however, there are six *non*-exhaustive 'considerations relevant to the weighing of hearsay evidence'.

First, whether it would have been reasonable, and practicable, for the party by whom the evidence was adduced to have produced the maker of the original statement as a witness. Secondly, whether the original statement was made contemporaneously with the occurrence, or existence of the matters stated. Thirdly, whether the evidence involves multiple hearsay.

Fourthly, whether any person involved had any *motive* to *conceal*, or to *misrepresent* matters. Fifthly, whether the original statement was an edited account, made in collaboration with another person, or for a particular purpose. Sixthly, whether the circumstances in which the evidence is adduced as hearsay are such as to suggest an *attempt* to *prevent* proper evaluation of its weight.

2. Practice

In practice, the fourth and sixth considerations are likely to be decisive.

In any event, *even if* there was not a *deliberate attempt* to prevent proper evaluation of the weight of a witness' evidence, if that witness does not undergo cross-examination, the *practical effect* is that a proper evaluation of the weight of that witness' evidence has, *in fact,* been prevented.

The first consideration can, perhaps, be somewhat allayed if all other parties are informed that a witness cannot attend a hearing, and the (good) reason for it, promptly.

c. Oral

A party who wishes to rely on a witness in relation to an issue of fact to be decided at a final hearing *must* serve a witness statement.

If a party has served a witness statement, and she wishes to rely at a hearing on the evidence of the author of that statement, she *must* also call that witness to give oral evidence. The main exception is where *notice* has been given that that witness will not attend.

Where a party ("A") knows that they are unable to attend, and notice has been provided to both the court, and to the other party ("B"), the court will decide the case in A's absence. Otherwise, the court may strike out a claim, defence, and counterclaim.

If it appears as though an essential witness for the other party has not attended, and that party is legally represented, politely enquire with the legal representative whether that witness has, in fact, attended. Dishonestly stating that a witness has attended, when an advocate *knows* that they have not, or *knows* that they *will not* attend, is unethical.

If you know that a witness has not attended, this will strengthen your client's negotiating position in relation to settlement.

i. Application to decide in absence

Where three conditions are met, if a party does not attend a hearing, the court *must* take into account that party's statement of case, and any other documents that she has filed and served, when the claim is decided (CPR 27.9).

First, *written notice* that the party will not attend has been given to the *court*, and to the other *party*, at least seven days before the final hearing. Secondly, at least seven days before the final hearing, any *other* documents which she has filed with the court are *served* on the other party. Thirdly, in the written notice, a *request* is made that the court decides the claim in her absence, and *compliance* with the first and second conditions are confirmed.

If these conditions are satisfied, there has been "written notice". The judge will then provide written reasons for the decision and send a copy to each party (PD 27 at [5.4]).

ii. Claimant

If a claimant does *not* attend the final hearing, and does *not* give written notice, the court may strike out the claim. Where the claim has been struck out, the claimant must apply for the order striking out the claim to be set aside, so that the claim can be heard (CPR 27.11).

iii. Defendant

The court may decide the claim on the basis of the claimant's evidence *alone*, provided that two conditions are met (CPR 27.9(3)).

First, the *defendant* does *not* attend the final hearing, *or* give written notice. Secondly, the *claimant* either *attends* the hearing, or gives written *notice*.

Where the *defence* has been struck out, the *defendant* must apply for the order striking out the claim to be set aside, so that the claim can be heard (CPR 27.11).

iv. Claimant & defendant

If *neither* party attends, *or* gives written notice, the court may strike out the claim, defence, and counterclaim (CPR 27.9(4)).

20. Independent & objective evidence

Standard directions in a claim following a road traffic collision usually order that documents and information sent to the court, and to each party, should, where possible, include plans, maps, photographs of the scene, and photographs of the damage. If possible, these should be agreed. A police accident report is also likely to assist the court, and standard directions usually order them to be filed, and served.

In principle, original documents must be brought to the hearing. In practice, however, legible photocopies are used, without recourse to originals, unless the copy is difficult to read.

a. Witnesses

An independent witness is likely to tip the balance where liability is in dispute arising from a road traffic collision, where she both writes a witness statement, and then attends court to give oral evidence. Either party can call an independent witness. What matters is that this witness is not *previously* known to either party, she expresses an opinion on who is at fault, and provides cogent reasons justifying her opinion.

b. Photographs

If a photograph was taken immediately after a road traffic collision, showing, for example, that the vehicles are touching, and that the defendant's vehicle is in the claimant's lane, this can be persuasive evidence that the defendant veered into the claimant's lane. Ideally, photographs should be exhibited to a witness statement, identifying *when* they were taken, by *whom*, and *what they show*. As the formal rules of evidence do not apply, however, a witness can give this evidence when examined in chief, or in cross-examination.

i. Clear

Photographs should be in colour.

Black and white photographs are often of poor quality. This is especially the case where they have been scanned or photocopied. It may be that the electronic version is in colour, but that the printer was set to black and white when the papers were printed. In any event, it is worth enquiring with your professional client whether colour photographs exist, so that they can be printed, given to the other side before the hearing, and relied on during the hearing.

ii. Location

In a claim following a road traffic collision, if there are no colour photographs of the location of the collision in the papers, consider using Google Maps. It is usually the case that a picture of the location can be found. If so, print off three colour copies.

If your client agrees that the photographs show the location of the collision in conference, speak to the other side to see if they concur. If they do, they will often be grateful to accept a colour copy, as will the court. If the other side does not agree that these photographs show the location of the collision, you will need to ask permission from the court to rely on them. Permission is likely to be granted, as evidence of the alleged location of the collision is likely to assist the court with, amongst other things, the road layout.

iii. Road layout

The number of lanes on a road, whether there were traffic lights, signs, and road markings should all be apparent from a photograph. There may also be an indication of the speed limit. For example, the presence of street lights generally means that there is a 30 mile per hour speed limit, unless otherwise specified (rule 124 of *The Highway Code*).

iv. Damage

Where liability is in dispute following a road traffic collision, colour photographs may show the detail, and the extent, of any damage. For example, whether the damage to the claimant's vehicle is a scratch, perhaps showing that the vehicles were moving at the point of impact. Or a large dent, perhaps showing that the collision could not properly be described as "low velocity". It may be possible to see the direction of impact from photographs of the damaged vehicles. This can chime with an engineer's report describing the direction of impact.

c. Sketch plans

Sketch plans are capable of assisting the court, especially where they are contemporaneous, detailed, and consistent with a party's statement of case, and witness evidence. Where there is a material inconsistency, however, this can be put in cross-examination, assisting, or undermining, a case. For example: the direction along the road that a vehicle was travelling; the lane that a vehicle was in; the location of the collision; mechanism of collision; and point of impact.

Ideally, sketch plans should be exhibited to a witness statement, identifying *when* they were taken, by *whom*, and *what they show*. As the formal rules of evidence do not apply, however, a witness can give this evidence when examined in chief, or in cross-examination.

d. Engineers' reports

An engineer's report provides the following eleven pieces of factual, and opinion evidence. The court usually needs an engineer's report in claims following a road traffic collision (PD 27 at Appendix A). The report should also contain a statement identifying who commissioned it, that the engineer understands her overriding duty to the court, and that she has in fact complied with that duty.

i. Collision

First, the date of the collision. Of course, if this is different to that pleaded in the statements of case, the written, or the oral evidence of a witness, it is either an error, or the report relates to damage that is unrelated to the index incident. Either way, this is an important inconsistency in a party's evidence, requiring an explanation from that party.

ii. Impact

Secondly, whether or not air bags deployed. If so, this suggests that the impact of a road traffic collision was considerable. In a claim for personal injury, it makes it more likely an occupant of that vehicle suffered more significant injury.

iii. Damage

Thirdly, the location of any damage. For example, 'moderate accidental damage to the right-hand side'. If this does not chime with what is pleaded in the statements of case, witness statements, or photographs after the collision, this is an important inconsistency.

Fourthly, vehicle history check. That is, whether there is a record of any adverse history. For example, isolated dents and scratches, and the effect that this has had on the pre-accident value.

iv. Value

Fifthly, the pre-accident value of the vehicle. This is likely to include: when the vehicle was first registered; the adjusted retail value for the vehicle of the relevant type and age; and trade value.

Sixthly, the cost of repair. This should include the *time* involved in conducting such repairs using Glass' Repair Estimate, and the *reasonable labour* charge, stating the rate per hour. The higher these are, the more likely it is that the damage is extensive, and that the collision was more significant. Any VAT should be set out.

Seventhly, the repair schedule, including the following: new parts required; parts that only require repainting; specialist and sundry charges, such as corrosion protection materials; and parts that require removal and refitting.

v. Write-off

Eighthly, whether the value, when compared to the cost of repair, means that it is uneconomical to repair. Ninthly, the salvage value. This is the value of parts that can be removed and sold, where the cost of repair exceeds the pre-accident value. So as to mitigate their loss, claimants are expected to offset this sum when claiming for repairs.

vi. Roadworthy

Tenthly, whether the vehicle is roadworthy. A typical sentence may read: 'In our opinion this vehicle was not roadworthy at the time of our inspection as a result of the damage sustained due to suspension damage'. Accordingly, in this circumstance, if towing and storage charges for a reasonable period are claimed, they are likely to be agreed, or allowed at a final hearing.

Eleventhly, whether *temporary* repairs would be *practical* to make the vehicle *roadworthy*. If so, this would *undermine* the need for a hire vehicle. If temporary repairs would *not* be practical, this would *establish* the need for a hire vehicle.

vii. Pictures

Pictures showing the vehicle are likely to be attached to the report. Of course, the registration plate should match the vehicle registration number set out in the report. Many pictures will be irrelevant, some will show the relevant damage, but, in any event, they should be in colour.

e. The Highway Code

The Highway Code is often essential for a final hearing, arising from a road traffic collision, where liability is in dispute. It is the starting point for identifying the standard of care that is expected of a reasonable driver. Section 38(7) of the Road Traffic Act 1988 provides that:

> A failure on the part of a person to observe a provision of the Highway Code shall not of itself render that person liable to criminal proceedings of any kind but any such failure may in any proceedings (whether civil or criminal, …) be relied upon by any party to the proceedings as tending to establish or negative any liability which is in question in those proceedings.

When relied on correctly, it can also be highly persuasive. It is not determinative, however, whether or not *The Highway Code* is evidence of negligence will depend very much on the circumstances. The majority of the Court of Appeal made this clear in *Goad v Butcher & Anor* [2011] EWCA Civ 158 at [9] (with emphasis added):

> "One can well understand the temptation in a case of this kind to place some emphasis on a breach of the Highway Code when it can be so clearly established, but in my view it was little more than an unfortunate red herring. A failure to observe the Code *may* be evidence of negligence, but whether it is will depend very much on the circumstances in which the act in question was committed and who is the claimant. …"

Lord Justice Jackson, dissenting from Moore-Bick and Mummery LJJ, said (with emphasis added) at paragraph 20 that:

"A breach of the Highway Code does *not* give rise to a presumption of negligence or constitute a breach of statutory duty. *It is, however, a relevant circumstance,* which the court should take into account when determining whether the driver was negligent: see *Powell v Phillips* [1972] 3 All ER 864."

In *Powell v Phillips* [1972] 3 All ER 864, [1973] RTR 19 at [22H-J], Lord Justice Stephenson (with whom Davies and Buckley LJJ agreed) said (with emphasis added) that:

"… It is, however, clear that a breach [of *The Highway Code*] creates no presumption of negligence calling for an explanation, still less a presumption of negligence making a real contribution to causing an accident or injury. The breach is *just one of the circumstances on which one party is entitled to rely* in establishing the negligence of the other and its contribution to causing the accident or injury. …"

f. Judicial College Guidelines

Where there is a claim for personal injury, the *Judicial College Guidelines for the Assessment of General Damages in Personal Injury Cases* (15th edn, OUP 2019) is essential (see chapter 27(h)). This new edition was published in November 2019.

It provides a clear and logical framework for the assessment of general damages in personal injury cases, takes into account inflation since the previous edition, and reflects the decisions of the higher courts on quantum. Chapter 13, 'Minor Injuries' is likely to provide most assistance in claims for personal injury that are allocated to the small claims track.

21. Submissions

When the parties invite the court to find in accordance with their case, this is known as "submissions". In cases that are allocated to the fast track, or to the multi-track, parties usually give *opening* submissions before witnesses are called to give oral evidence. This is unusual in a claim that has been allocated to the small claims track. It follows that *closing* submissions are even more important; they provide a final opportunity to influence the judgment.

a. Opening

There is usually no need for opening submissions. The fact that a case has been allocated to the small claims track *should* mean that there are no complicated issues of law or fact. One of the parties usually lists the issues that are agreed, the issues that are in dispute, and whether or not there are any preliminary applications before the final hearing (see chapter 17).

b. Closing

The court may adopt any method of proceeding that is considered to be fair (CPR 27.8(1) and chapter 18). It may be, however, that the court does not wish to hear from a party ("A") at the conclusion of a hearing. If that is the party who you represent, excellent. It is usually an indication that the *other* party ("B") has not (yet) persuaded the court of B's case, as it would not normally be just to dismiss B's case without hearing submissions from B.

i. Order

The claimant usually has the last word, as it is the claimant's case. Accordingly, the defendant is often asked to give closing submissions first. *Claimants* are therefore at an advantage for two reasons. First, they can take a careful note of the *defendant's* submissions, and thereby incorporate any response into the *claimant's* submissions. Secondly, there is not usually an opportunity for the *defendant* to reply to the *claimant's* submissions.

ii. Approach to fact-finding

To use Mr Justice Stewart's words in *Kimathi & Ors v The Foreign & Commonwealth Office* [2018] EWHC 2066 (QB) ("*Kimathi*") at [95], there are three judgments which have "helpfully crystallised and advanced learning in respect of the approach to evidence."

First, *Gestmin SGPS SA v Credit Suisse (UK) Ltd & Anor* [2013] EWHC 3560 (Comm). Secondly, *Lachaux v Lachaux* [2017] EWHC 385 (Fam), [2017] 4 WLR 57. Thirdly, *Carmarthenshire County Council v Y* [2017] EWFC 36. Thankfully, Stewart J summarised the key principles in *Kimathi* at paragraph 96 in these terms:

"i) *Gestmin*:

- We believe memories to be more faithful than they are. Two common errors are to suppose (1) that the stronger and more vivid the recollection, the more likely it is to be accurate; (2) the more confident another person is in their recollection, the more likely it is to be accurate.

- Memories are fluid and malleable, being constantly rewritten whenever they are retrieved. This is even true of 'flash bulb' memories (a misleading term), i.e. memories of experiencing or learning of a particularly shocking or traumatic event.

- Events can come to be recalled as memories which did not happen at all or which happened to somebody else.

- The process of civil litigation itself subjects the memories of witnesses to powerful biases.

- Considerable interference with memory is introduced in civil litigation by the procedure of preparing for trial. Statements are often taken a long time after relevant events and drafted by a lawyer who is conscious of the significance for the issues in the case of what the witness does or does not say.

- The best approach from a judge is to base factual findings on inferences drawn from documentary evidence and known or probable facts. 'This does not mean that oral testimony serves no useful purpose… But its value lies largely… in the opportunity which cross-examination affords to subject the documentary record to critical scrutiny and to gauge the personality, motivations and working practices of a witness, rather than in testimony of what the witness recalls of particular conversations and events. Above all, it is important to avoid the fallacy of supposing that, because a witness has confidence in his or her recollection and is honest, evidence based on that recollection provides any reliable guide to the truth'.

ii) *Lachaux*:

- Mostyn J cited extensively from *Gestmin* and referred to two passages in earlier authorities. I extract from those citations, and from Mostyn J's judgment, the following:

- 'Witnesses, especially those who are emotional, who think they are morally in the right, tend very easily and unconsciously to conjure up a legal right that did not exist. It is a truism, often used in accident cases, that with every day that passes the memory becomes fainter and the imagination becomes more active. For that reason, a witness, however honest, rarely persuades a judge that his present recollection is preferable to that which was taken down in writing immediately after the incident occurred. Therefore, contemporary documents are always of the utmost importance…'

- '…I have found it essential in cases of fraud, when considering the credibility of witnesses, always to test their veracity by reference to the objective fact proved independently of their testimony, in particular by reference to the documents in the case, and also to pay particular regard to their motives and to the overall probabilities...'

- Mostyn J said of the latter quotation, 'these wise words are surely of general application and are not confined to fraud cases... it is certainly often difficult to tell whether a witness is telling the truth and I agree with the view of Bingham J that the demeanour of a witness is not a reliable pointer to his or her honesty.'

iii) *Carmarthenshire County Council*:

- The general rule is that oral evidence given under cross-examination is the gold standard because it reflects the long-established common law consensus that the best way of assessing the reliability of evidence is by confronting the witness.

- However, oral evidence under cross-examination is far from the be all and end all of forensic proof. Referring to paragraph 22 of *Gestmin*, Mostyn J said:

> '...this approach applies equally to all fact-finding exercises, especially where the facts in issue are in the distant past. This approach does not dilute the importance that the law places on cross-examination as a vital component of due process, but it does place it in its correct context.'"

iii. Credibility

At paragraph 98 in *Kimathi*, Mr Justice Stewart continued by endorsing the late Lord Bingham's approach to assessing the credibility of witnesses: there are "three main tests which in general give a useful pointer as to where the truth lies, although their relative importance will vary from case to case". First, consistency with agreed facts. Secondly, internal consistency. Thirdly, consistency with what has previously been asserted.

1. Agreed facts

Agreed facts provide the court with an *anchor* from which the judge can build a picture as to what happened. Where a witness gives evidence that is disputed, but consistent with *agreed* or *known* facts, it is likely to be given significant weight. Where her account is *in*consistent with the same, however, it is *un*likely to be given much weight, and that witness' credibility is likely to diminish accordingly.

It follows that it is useful to demonstrate three circumstances.

First, *to what extent* a party's ("A") *evidence* is consistent with *agreed* and *known* facts. Secondly, how *near* to the safe, judicial ground of agreed and known facts A's *case* is. Thirdly, how *far* it is from this safe ground to the other party's ("B") case.

2. Internal inconsistency

Where a party's case is not internally consistent, it is helpful to demonstrate the reasons *why*.

For example, if a party's statement of case pleads X, but that party's witness and oral evidence *also* confirm the truth of Y, and X and Y are incompatible, that party's case appears to be *internally* inconsistent. If this party is the claimant, who has the burden of proving that what is pleaded in their statement of case is more likely than not, then, this can be a persuasive submission, after which the court can confidently dismiss the claim.

For example, the claimant's particulars of claim plead that the mechanism of collision was a rear-end shunt. Yet the claimant's *written* evidence confirms that the impact was to the left, passenger-side of her vehicle. There may also be *objective* evidence of the same.

For example, an engineer's report, that has photographs attached, confirming that the damage to the claimant's vehicle is to the left, passenger-side. The claimant's *oral* evidence (answers in cross-examination), may also evidence that the damage was to the left, passenger-side of her vehicle.

In these circumstances, the mechanism of collision pleaded in the statement of case is *in*compatible with the claimant's evidence, and other, objective (photographic) evidence. If follows that the claimant's case is *internally in*consistent. As the claimant has the burden of proving, on a balance of probabilities, that the collision occurred in accordance with her statement of case, and she has failed to do so, her case will be dismissed.

3. Consistent previous statements

There are at least seven indicators of unsatisfactory witness evidence that are apparent in the judgment of Mr Justice Lewison (as he then was) in *Painter v Hutchison & Anor* [2007] EWHC 758 (Ch)at [3].

Where an indicator applies, it may also be indicative that a witness has been *in*consistent. Where no such indicators apply, however, it may be indicative that a witness has been *con*sistent. In either case, indicators below can be used in closing submissions as a useful pointer as to where the truth lies.

First, evasive and argumentative answers. Secondly, tangential speeches, avoiding the question. Thirdly, blaming legal advisers for documentation, such as statements of case, and witness statements. Fourthly, self-contradiction. Fifthly, internal inconsistency. Sixthly, shifting case. Seventhly, introducing new evidence.

If none of these indicators apply to your witness, it may be helpful to *show* that. Likewise, if one or more of these indicators apply to the other party's witness, that may also be worth *showing* to the court. It is usually more persuasive to *show* the court *how* a witness contradicted her evidence in cross-examination, for example, rather than merely *tell* the court. This is because the court is able to come to the same conclusion *of its own accord.*

An accurate note of the hearing can be invaluable (see chapter 26). With it, you are able to *quote* the witness *in her own words*, rather than merely *paraphrase*. You are also able to *show* that the witness said *X* at the beginning of cross-examination, yet she said *Y* at the close of it, and thereby changed her position. X and Y are incompatible. Y is in accordance with your client's case. Further, the words that you quote may chime with the court's note of what was said for maximum impact.

iv. Inherent unlikelihood

Where there is inherent unlikelihood in what is pleaded in a statement of case, stated in a witness statement, or oral evidence, this is usually worth demonstrating to the court. This is often the least persuasive argument, however, so, prioritise your time with your strongest points, and, *if there is time*, demonstrate the inherent unlikelihood of the other party's case.

22. Orders & judgment

An "order" may be made without a judgment, whereas, a "judgment" is usually followed by an order. Confusingly, however, "judgment" and "order" are used throughout the CPRs interchangeably, and, at other times, in conjunction.

a. Orders

Judgments and orders are usually made by the court. The parties can draw up draft orders, however, including those that are attached to applications, proposed consent orders before judgment, and draft minutes of order following judgment.

i. Carriage

The court usually draws up an order after disposing of a claim, or deciding an application, in a claim that was allocated to the small claims track, however, a party may be asked to draw up an order (CPR 40.3(1)(a)). If so, the party who has brought the claim, or made the application, will have "carriage" of the order. If only one of the parties is represented, however, that party will be directed to draw up the order.

In principle, where an order is drawn up by a party, it must be filed no later than seven days after the date on which the court so ordered (CPR 40.3(3)(a)). In practice, orders should be drawn up on the day of the hearing, and, in any event, no later than 24 hours after the hearing.

If requested to draw up the order, get the court's (or the judge's) email address from the usher. From time-to-time, the court may insist that a handwritten copy of a minute of order is handed to an usher, rather than that an electronic version is emailed to the court. For this reason, it is a good idea to carry an A4, lined notepad. Writing should be in black ink, and text should be in capital letters, so that, when scanned, and photocopied, it remains legible.

ii. Consent

Where the parties have settled a claim, or an application has been agreed, before the court has given a decision on the same, the parties should draw up a "consent" order. Where a party is *un*represented, judicial approval is always necessary (CPR 40.6(2)(b)).

There are three requirements (CPR 40.6(7) and PD 40B at [3.4]). First, it must be drawn up in the terms that have been agreed. Secondly, it must be expressed as being "by consent". Thirdly, it must be signed by the legal representatives acting for the parties (or, if a party is in person, by that person).

iii. Tomlin

Parties who have settled their dispute may wish to set out the terms that have been agreed, otherwise than in the consent order itself. As court orders are public documents, a "Tomlin" order is useful where the parties wish the terms of their agreement to remain confidential. It stays all further proceedings on the terms that have been agreed.

There are two main ways to record these terms. First, in a schedule following the order. Secondly, in a settlement agreement, attached to the order. The parties are entitled to apply to the court to enforce these terms, should that be necessary.

The Tomlin order itself (as opposed to the schedule, or the settlement agreement) should provide for *costs*. For example, payment and assessment of costs, each party to bear their own costs, or no order as to costs.

Where there has been agreement for the payment and assessment of costs, there are three benefits of including this in the Tomlin order itself. First, there is a judgment for costs. Secondly, interest will accrue. Thirdly, there is right to a detailed assessment.

The court is reluctant to go behind what the parties have agreed.

iv. Unless

An "unless" order which requires an act to be done must specify the time within which the act should be done. The exception is a judgment or order for the payment of an amount of money. The consequences of failure to do so may be set out in the order. If so, the following, suitably adapted wording must be used, wherever possible (PD 40B at [8.2(1)]):

> Unless the [claimant][defendant] [files and serves] [an amended, fully particularised] [particulars of claim][defence] by 4.00pm on Friday, 25 October 2019 his [claim][defence] will be struck out and judgment entered for the [defendant][claimant].

b. Judgment

In general, "judgment" is a final, reasoned decision of the court, determining whether a claim is allowed, or dismissed. It takes effect when it is made. That is, when declared, or announced.

i. Default

"Default judgment" is the determination of a claim following a party's failure to file an acknowledgment of service, defence, or defence to counterclaim, within the relevant time limit (see chapter 17(a)).

ii. After final hearing

In principle, judgment may be given after the date of the final hearing. In practice, this is rare.

1. Ex tempore

Judgment in a claim that is allocated to the small claims track is usually given orally, immediately after the hearing. This is known as an "ex tempore" judgment. It is important to take a careful note for four reasons.

First, to identify if there are any grounds of appeal. Secondly, to advise on prospects of successfully appealing. Thirdly, so that both your professional client, and your lay client, are able to reflect on the reasoning of the judgment. Fourthly, as transcripts of proceedings are unnecessary to appeal a judgment from a claim that was allocated to the small claims track (see chapter 25(c)(iv)(4)).

2. Reserved

Occasionally, judgment will be "reserved". This may be the case where there is an exceptionally large amount of material for the judge to digest, authority that the court wishes to consider in its own time, or where there is insufficient time. A reserved judgment may be given orally, at a later hearing, or in writing.

iii. Slip rule

Once a judgment has been entered, the decision cannot be reconsidered. The sole exception is to correct an accidental slip, or omission under the "slip rule" (CPR 40.12(1)). A party may apply for an error in a judgment, or an order to be corrected, without giving notice to the other party (PD·40B at [4.1]).

The application notice should describe the error and set out the required correction. This may be done through an informal document, such as a letter. The application may be considered without a hearing in three circumstances.

First, the application so requests. Secondly, with the consent of the parties. Thirdly, where the court does not consider that a hearing would be appropriate.

If the slip is *obvious*, the court may deal with the application without notice, or direct that notice of the application is served on the other party. If the application is opposed, it should, if practicable, be listed for a hearing before the judge who gave judgment or made the order. The court has an inherent power to vary its orders, to make the *meaning*, and the *intention* of the court clear (PD 40B at [4.5]).

iv. Reasons

The court *must* give reasons for its decision (CPR 27.8(6)).

1. Duty

The court owes a *general duty* to give reasons.

In *Flannery & Anor v Halifax Estate Agencies Ltd* [1999] EWCA Civ 811, [2000] WLR 377, 381-382, the Court of Appeal gave four pieces of practical guidance, which deserve to be quoted in full:

"(1) The duty is a function of due process, and therefore of justice. Its rationale has two principal aspects. The first is that fairness surely requires that the parties especially the losing party should be left in no doubt why they have won or lost. This is especially so since without reasons the losing party will not know ... whether the court has misdirected itself, and thus whether he may have an available appeal on the substance of the case. The second is that a requirement to give reasons concentrates the mind; if it is fulfilled, the resulting decision is much more likely to be soundly based on the evidence than if it is not.

(2) The first of these aspects implies that want of reasons may be a good self-standing ground of appeal. Where because no reasons

are given it is impossible to tell whether the judge has gone wrong on the law or the facts, the losing party would be altogether deprived of his chance of an appeal unless the court entertains an appeal based on the lack of reasons itself.

(3) The extent of the duty, or rather the reach of what is required to fulfil it, depends on the subject matter. Where there is a straightforward factual dispute whose resolution depends simply on which witness is telling the truth about events which he claims to recall, it is likely to be enough for the judge (having, no doubt, summarised the evidence) to indicate simply that he believes X rather than Y; indeed there may be nothing else to say. But where the dispute involves something in the nature of an intellectual exchange, with reasons and analysis advanced on either side, the judge must enter into the issues canvassed before him and explain why he prefers one case over the other. This is likely to apply particularly in litigation where as here there is disputed expert evidence; but it is not necessarily limited to such cases.

(4) This is not to suggest that there is one rule for cases concerning the witnesses truthfulness or recall of events, and another for cases where the issue depends on reasoning or analysis (with experts or otherwise). The rule is the same: the judge must explain *why* he has reached his decision. The question is always, what is required of the judge to do so; and that will differ from case to case. Transparency should be the watchword."

Without reasons, a judgment is not transparent. An appeal court cannot know whether or not the judge had adequate reasons for the conclusion reached. Reasons may be as *brief,* and as *simple*, as the nature of the case allows. Normally, they will be given at the end of the hearing, however, the court may do so at another hearing, either orally, or in writing (PD 27 at [5.3]).

2. Note

A note of the reasons will be sent to each party in two situations (PD 27 at [5.4]). First, a case decided without a hearing. Secondly, a party who does not attend a hearing, but has given notice (as prescribed in CPR 27.9(1)).

3. Failure

Where permission to appeal – due to lack of reasons – is made out immediately after judgment, *English v Emery Reimbold & Strick Ltd* [2002] EWCA Civ 605, [2002] 3 All ER 385 at [25] prescribes the procedure to follow (with emphasis added):

> "… the Judge should consider whether his judgment is defective for lack of reasons, adjourning for that purpose should he find this necessary. If he concludes that it is, *he should set out to remedy the defect by the provision of additional reasons refusing permission to appeal on the basis that he has adopted that course.* If he concludes that he has given adequate reasons, he will no doubt refuse permission to appeal. If an application for permission to appeal on the ground of lack of reasons is made to the appellate court and it appears to the appellate court that the application is well founded, it should consider adjourning the application and remitting the case to the trial Judge with an invitation to provide additional reasons for his decision or, where appropriate, his reasons for a specific finding or findings. Where the appellate court is in doubt as to whether the reasons are adequate, it may be appropriate to direct that the application be adjourned to an oral hearing, on notice to the respondent."

v. Reconsideration

An application for permission to appeal may be well-founded where there are any of the following four failures.

First, to identify the elements of the claim or defence. Secondly, to analyse contemporary documents. Thirdly, to deal with the thrust of expert evidence. Fourthly, to take a balanced approach to assessing the credibility of witnesses of fact.

In *Simetra Global Assets Ltd & Anor v Ikon Finance Ltd & Ors* [2019] EWCA Civ 1413, [2019] 4 WLR 112 at [46], Lord Justice Males (with whom Peter Jackson and McCombe LJJ agreed) gave the following guidance (with emphasis added):

> "First, succinctness is as desirable in a judgment as it is in counsel's submissions, but *short judgments must be careful judgments*. Second, it is not necessary to deal expressly with every point, but a judge must say enough to show that care has been taken and that the evidence as a whole has been properly considered. Which points need to be dealt with and which can be omitted itself requires an exercise of judgment. Third, the best way to demonstrate the exercise of the necessary care is to make use of 'the building blocks of the reasoned judicial process' by identifying the issues which need to be decided, marshalling (however briefly and without needing to recite every point) the evidence which bears on those issues, and giving reasons why the principally relevant evidence is either accepted or rejected as unreliable. Fourth, and in particular, fairness requires that a judge should deal with apparently compelling evidence, where it exists, which is contrary to the conclusion which he proposes to reach and explain why he does not accept it."

In the next paragraph, Lord Justice Males said that failure to follow this guidance does not *necessarily* mean that a judgment is inadequately reasoned, however, "the judgment will need to be particularly cogent if it is to satisfy the demands of justice." This is because of the risk that an appellate court will conclude that the judge has plainly failed to take the evidence into account.

vi. Appeals

Section 80 of the County Courts Act 1984 is not affected (PD 27 at [5.5]).

1. Note

This section provides that a party may request that a judge notes three points. First, any question of law raised at the hearing. Secondly, the facts in evidence in relation to any such question. Thirdly, her decision on any such question, and of her determination of the proceedings.

2. Signed copy

The judge must provide a signed copy of this note where the following two conditions are met. First, a party has made an application. Secondly, the relevant fee has been paid. (It is *irrelevant* whether a notice of appeal has been served.) This note must be used at the hearing of the appeal.

c. Time limits for compliance

The general rule is that, unless the court orders otherwise, the time limit for complying with a judgment or an order is within 14 days (CPR 40.11). The date for compliance must be expressed as a calendar date. It must also include the time of day by which the act must be done (CPR 2.9(1)).

23. Costs, disbursements & witness expenses

The general rule is that there are "no costs" in claims that are allocated to the small claims track. The exception is where the court finds that one party has behaved unreasonably (see chapter 24(a)). Usually, costs that can be recovered from the other party after a successful claim that was allocated to the small claims track can be determined in advance of issue.

a. General discretion

As night follows day, costs do *not* always follow the event.

It is correct that, *if* the court decides to make an order about costs, the *general rule* is that the *un*successful party will be ordered to pay the costs of the *successful* party. But the court may make a different order (CPR 44.2(2)). The court has a *general* discretion, which can be broken down into the following three *particular* discretions (CPR 44.2(1)).

First, *whether* costs are payable by one party to another. Secondly, the *amount* of those costs. Thirdly, *when* they are to be paid.

i. Payable

The costs rule in relation to *claims that are allocated to the small claims track* does not fetter this general discretion. It provides that 'the court may not order a party to pay a sum to another party in respect of that other party's costs, fees and expenses …' (CPR 27.14(2)). This rule does *not* prescribe that the court *will* order those costs to be paid by an unsuccessful defendant; it provides that the court *may* order those costs to be paid.

It follows that a defendant who has been unsuccessful after a final hearing can still argue that the court should not make an order for costs. To do so, the court should be invited to have regard to all the circumstances. In particular, the following three (CPR 44.2(4)).

First, the *conduct* of the parties. Secondly, whether a party has succeeded on *part* of its case, even if that party has not been wholly successful. Thirdly, any admissible *offer* to settle made by a party, which is drawn to the court's attention.

1. Conduct

In particular, conduct of a party includes the following four circumstances (CPR 44.2(5)).

First, conduct *before*, as well as *during*, the proceedings, and in particular the *extent* to which the parties followed the Practice Direction – Pre-Action Conduct, or any relevant pre-action protocol (see appendix E). Secondly, whether it was reasonable for a party to *raise*, *pursue*, or *contest* a particular allegation or issue.

Thirdly, the *manner* in which a party has pursued, or defended its case, or a particular allegation or issue. Fourthly, whether a claimant who has succeeded in the claim, in whole or in part, *exaggerated* its claim.

Even where a defendant's submission that a party has behaved unreasonably is unsuccessful, the same factors can be used to argue that the conduct of the claimant is such that the court should not award fixed costs (see chapter 23(a)(i)).

2. Limited success

Where a claimant has claimed £8,000 in respect of three heads of loss, for example, yet the court dismisses two of those heads of loss, and allows one for £3,000, the claimant has had "limited success". In principle, there is an argument that the defendant should not have to pay the claimant's costs, as she has had *such* limited success. In practice, the court is likely to award the claimant's costs, but, perhaps, reduce the amount (see below).

3. Offers

Rejection of an offer in settlement will not, *of itself*, amount to behaving unreasonably (CPR 27.14(3)). It may well be a good reason to submit that the defendant should not have to pay the claimant's fixed costs, however, where that offer was made *early* in proceedings, for example, and for an amount *significantly greater* than that awarded following a final hearing.

ii. Amount

If the court decides that, *in principle*, the defendant should pay the claimant's costs, that is not the end of the matter. The court still has a discretion as to the *amount* of those costs.

A simple submission is that if, say, £8,000 was claimed, yet £3,000 was in fact awarded: the appropriate issue fee (if issued online) is £105 (as opposed to £410); and the appropriate hearing fee is £170 (as opposed to £335).

iii. When

The general rule is that, unless the court orders otherwise, the time limit for payment of costs is within 14 days (CPR 40.11). The court has discretion, however, to order payment within 21 days, for example, where a defendant has limited means, and invites the court to order payment within a longer period of time.

b. Fees

Issue, hearing, and application fees are payable by the party who starts a claim, requires a final hearing to determine that claim, and makes an application. A party is entitled to apply for help with these fees where they have limited means, or they are on a low income.

i. Issue

To start a claim, a claim form (or counterclaim) must be "issued" with the court. This can either be done online, or by using paper copies. The former is cheaper, however, if you do not know the exact amount that you are claiming, it cannot be issued online.

The correct fee can be found online by searching for 'Make a court claim for money' at www.gov.uk. The issue fee is based on the "amount claimed". This *includes any interest* that is also claimed. To calculate five percent of the value of the claim, take the value of the claim, and multiply it by 0.05, and round the sum to the nearest penny.

The following are correct as of 1 November 2019:

Amount claimed	Issue fee	
	Paper	Online
Not more than £300	£35	£25
£300.01 to £500	£50	£35
£500.01 to £1,000	£70	£60
£1,000.01 to £1,500	£80	£70
£1,500.01 to £3,000	£115	£105
£3,000.01 to £5,000	£205	£185
£5,000.01 to £10,000	£455	£410
£10,000.01 to £100,000	5% of the claim	4.5% of the claim

ii. Hearing

Paragraph 1 at 2.1 of Schedule 1 of the Civil Proceedings Order 2008 (SI 2008/1058) prescribes the relevant hearing fee. The following are correct as of 1 November 2019:

Amount claimed	Hearing fee
Not more than £300	£25
£300.01 to £500	£55
£500.01 to £1,000	£80
£1,000.01 to £1,500	£115
£1,500.01 to £3,000	£170
More than £3,000	£335

iii. Application

Fees payable on applications are set out in Form EX 50, valid from March 2019.

1. On notice

Where there is notification of the application served on the other party, the fee is £155.

2. Consent

Where an application is made by consent, without notice, and no other fee is specified (for example, to vacate, or to adjourn a hearing), the fee is £50.

3. Permission to appeal

On filing an appellant's notice, or filing a respondent's notice, the fee is £120.

iv. Remission

A claimant can apply for help with court fees. This is called "fee remission" (see chapter 6(k)).

c. Legal representatives

Claimants can recover "fixed costs" attributable to issuing a claim which are (or would be) payable under Part 45 (if that part applied to the claim) (CPR 27.14(2)(a)). Part 45 is concerned with amounts which are to be allowed in respect of *legal representatives'* charges, as opposed to litigants in person, or lay representatives' charges (CPR 45.1(1)).

i. Specified sum

Where the claim is for a specified sum of money, and a legal representative drafted the claim, the fixed commencement costs are prescribed in CPR 45.2, Table 1. The following are correct as of 1 November 2019:

Amount claimed	Claim form served by the court, or by any method other than personal service by the claimant	Claim form served personally by the claimant	
		One defendant	For each additional defendant personally served at separate addresses
£25 to £500	£50	£60	£15
£500 to £1,000	£70	£80	£15
£1,000 to £5,000; or the only claim is for delivery of goods, and no value is specified on the claim form	£80	£90	£15
More than £5,000	£100	£110	£15

ii. Unspecified sum

Where the sum that is claimed is unspecified, fixed costs will be calculated by reference to the judgment sum awarded after a final hearing, and CPR 45.2, Table 1 (see above).

iii. Counterclaim

There are no fixed costs on a counterclaim.

iv. Injunction

A party *may* be ordered to pay a sum not exceeding £260 for legal advice and assistance in claims including an injunction, or specific performance (PD 27 at [7.2]).

d. Party or witness

The court may award a party, or a witness, loss of earnings, or loss of leave, and travel expenses. These may be claimed by a claimant, or by a defendant. Loss of earnings, and travel expenses can be usually be agreed, subject to liability.

i. Loss of earnings

The court may award a sum not exceeding £95 for any loss of earnings, or loss of leave by a party, or witness, due to attending a hearing, or to staying away from home for the purposes of attending a hearing (CPR 27.14(2)(e) and PD 27 at [7.3]).

1. Employed

Where a witness is employed, and the final hearing is listed and heard in the morning, loss of earnings based on an hourly rate can be calculated. Where the case is on a floating list, however, and the matter goes into the afternoon, the daily rate will be appropriate. The court is also able to compensate a witness who has taken leave to attend a hearing.

2. Self-employed

The key question is whether a self-employed witness was *required* or *lost an opportunity* to work. If so, it may be claimed. For example, a driver who has set hours, or a beautician who lost an appointment. Where a driver is able to work at any time, however, it is harder to submit that this person lost earnings *due to attending a hearing.*

3. Other

An expense of staying away from home may include the cost of, for example, a carer to look after an elderly dependent, so that the witness is able to attend a hearing.

ii. Travel expenses

The court may award the expenses that a party, or witness has *reasonably* incurred in travelling to, and from, a hearing, or staying away from home *for the purpose of attending a hearing* (CPR 27.14(2)(d)). This includes the amount paid for parking, and an amount for use of a private car.

Usually, a witness travels from the postcode set out in her witness statement, so that the mileage to court can be calculated online, by searching for directions from that postcode to the court. If the witness is going to drive home, then the mileage is doubled, and, by convention, multiplied by 0.45 to work out the amount in pounds. This is the expense of private car use, which includes, for example, fuel, a share of wear and tear, expendables, and tax.

There are two key arguments here. First, the amount claimed for travel expenses is not *reasonable*. Secondly, those expenses were not *solely* for the purpose of attending a hearing.

1. Reasonable

Where travel expenses appear to be unusually high, a suspiciously round figure, or both, a party can request to see evidence of these expenses. Even if this evidence is provided, there may be a possibility of useful cross-examination.

For example, if a successful claimant has claimed the cost of staying the night in a Central London hotel, so as to attend a final hearing at the County Court at Central London, yet she lives in Central London, the court may not regard this as reasonable.

2. Purpose

If a witness drove *in*directly to the final hearing, for example, because she wanted to pick something up from work along the journey, then this part of the journey is not claimable. That witness would have to make the journey to pick up that item anyway; it is not for the purpose of attending a hearing.

e. Expert

The court may award a sum not exceeding £750 for an expert's fees (CPR 27.14(2)(f) and PD 27 at [7.3]).

f. Lay representative

The limits on costs also apply to any fee or reward charged by a person exercising a right of audience by a lay representative (CPR 27.14(4)).

g. Personal injury

Stage 1 fixed costs, and, where relevant, Stage 2 fixed costs under CPR 45.18 may be claimed where the following criteria are satisfied.

First, the claim was within the scope of the Pre-Action Protocol for Low Value Personal Injury Claims in Road Traffic Accidents, or the Pre-Action Protocol for Low Value Personal Injury (Employers' Liability and Public Liability) Claims. Secondly, the claimant reasonably believed that the claim was valued at more than the small claims track limit, in accordance with the relevant protocol. Thirdly, the defendant did not pay those Stage 1 and, where relevant, Stage 2 fixed costs.

h. Appeal

The costs regime for cases allocated to the small claims track applies to the costs of an appeal (*Akhtar v Boland (Costs)* [2014] EWCA Civ 943, [2014] CP Rep 41 at [7]).

i. Re-allocation

Where a claim has been reallocated to another track from the small claims track, or to the small claims track from another track, there are separate rules.

i. After leaving the small claims track

Small claims track costs do *not* apply *after* the date that the claim has been reallocated to another track. The rules that apply to the *new* track will apply (CPR 27.15).

ii. Before re-allocation to the small claims track

The rules that apply to the track *before* reallocation apply up to the *date of reallocation*. The rules that apply to the small claims track will apply *thereafter*, unless the court orders otherwise (CPR 46.13(2)).

24. Unreasonable behaviour

Where the court finds that a party has "behaved unreasonably", in principle, the innocent party may recover their costs. It is, in some cases, of *singular* importance, *especially* where the amount in dispute is eclipsed, in real terms, by the cost of defending a claim.

a. Disapplication of fixed costs

The court may not order a party to pay a sum to another party in respect of costs, fees and expenses (including those relating to an appeal), except 'such further costs as the court may assess by the summary procedure and order to be paid by a party who has behaved unreasonably' (CPR 27.14(2)(g)).

b. Definition

There is no definition in the CPR of "behaved unreasonably". Accordingly, we can look to authority for guidance; and the dictionary, as a well-established aid to statutory interpretation.

i. Authority

The following authorities provide guidance on the phrases "behaved unreasonably", "unreasonable", and "unreasonable conduct". It is the first, of course, that is authoritative.

1. Behaved unreasonably

In *Dammermann v Lanyon Bowder LLP* [2017] EWCA Civ 269, [2017] 2 Costs LR 393 ("*Dammermann*"), Longmore and McFarlane LJJ gave the following guidance (with emphasis added):

"30. ... We doubt if we can usefully give general guidance in relation to the circumstances in which it will be appropriate for a court to decide whether a party 'has behaved unreasonably' since *all such cases must be highly fact-sensitive.* In the somewhat different context of the jurisdiction to order a party's legal (or other) representative to meet what are called 'wasted costs' (defined as costs incurred 'as a result of any improper, unreasonable or negligent act or omission' of such representative), the court speaking through Sir Thomas Bingham MR said:

> 'conduct cannot be described as unreasonable simply because it leads in the event to an unsuccessful result or because other more cautious legal representatives would have acted differently. *The acid test is whether the conduct permits of a reasonable explanation.* If so, the course adopted may be regarded as optimistic and as reflecting in a practitioner's judgment, but it is not unreasonable.'

See *Ridehalgh v Horsefield [1994] Ch 205*, 232F.

31. While we would not wish to incorporate all the learning about wasted costs orders into decisions under CPR Part 27.14(2)(g), we think that *the above dictum should give sufficient guidance on the word 'unreasonably' to district judges and circuit judges dealing with cases allocated to the Small Claims Track. Ridehalgh was, of course, dealing with acts or omissions of legal representatives but the meaning of 'unreasonably' cannot be different when applied to litigants in person in small claims cases. Litigants in person should not be in a better position than legal representatives but neither should they be in any worse position than such representatives.*

32. The only other thing we can usefully add is that it would be unfortunate if litigants were too easily deterred from using the Small Claims Track by the risk of being held to have behaved unreasonably and thus rendering themselves liable for costs. ..."

This guidance can be summarised into three key points.

First, all cases are highly fact-sensitive. Secondly, the acid test is whether the conduct permits of a reasonable explanation. Thirdly, the meaning of 'unreasonably' cannot be different when applied to litigants in person.

Recently, in *Gempride Ltd v Bamrah & Anor* [2018] EWCA Civ 1367, [2019] 1 WLR 1545 at [26], Lord Justice Hickinbottom (with whom Lord Justice Davis agreed) provided five further points of guidance on the wasted cost jurisdiction and *Ridehalgh*.

First, *mistake, error of judgment*, or *negligence*, without more, will be insufficient to amount to unreasonable conduct. Secondly, although the conduct of the relevant legal representative *must* amount to a breach of duty owed by that representative to the court, the conduct does *not* have to be in breach of any formal professional rule, or amount to dishonesty.

Thirdly, the burden of proof lies on the *applicant*, in the sense that the court cannot make a finding, unless it is satisfied that the behaviour was "unreasonable". Fourthly, even where the threshold criteria are satisfied, the court *still* has a discretion as to whether to make an order. Fifthly, if the court determines that there has been "unreasonable behaviour", the sanction must be *proportionate to the misconduct as found*, in all the circumstances.

2. Unreasonable

In *Associated Provincial Picture Houses Ltd v Wednesbury Corp* [1947] 2 All ER 680, 682-683, the then Master of the Rolls famously said (with emphasis added):

> "Lawyers familiar with the phraseology commonly used in relation to the exercise of statutory discretions often use the word 'unreasonable' in a rather comprehensive sense. It is frequently used as a general description of the things that must not be done. For instance, a person entrusted with a discretion must direct himself properly in law. He must call his own attention to the

matters which he is bound to consider. He must exclude from his consideration matters which are irrelevant to the matters that he had to consider. *If he does not obey the rules, he may truly be said, and often is said, to be acting 'unreasonably'.*"

3. Unreasonable conduct

In *Croydon v Greenham (Plant Hire) Ltd* [1978] ICR 415, the Employment Appeal Tribunal ("EAT") considered section 21(1) of the Employment Appeal Tribunal Rules 1976, which was as follows (with emphasis added):

Where it appears to the appeal tribunal that any proceedings were unnecessary, improper or vexatious, or that there has been unreasonable delay or other *unreasonable conduct* in bringing or conducting the proceedings, the tribunal may order the party at fault to pay to any other party the whole or such part as it thinks fit of the costs or expenses incurred by that other party in connection with the proceedings.

At 417-418, the EAT reasoned (with emphasis added) that:

"Another basic feature of the jurisdiction of the industrial tribunals and the appeal tribunal is that it is only in exceptional circumstances defined in the appropriate rules that we are empowered to award costs to the successful party. *The award of costs, when appropriate, is primarily with the object of minimising the financial detriment to the successful partywhich has occurred by reason of him being made a party to the proceedings by the unsuccessful party.* But there is another element which is also important: *it is only by the award of costs against the unsuccessful litigant that you have any safeguard at all against completely irresponsible litigation.* One of the reasons why, in England, there is less irresponsible litigation than under some systems is that in the superior courts in England, if you lose you have to pay the other side's costs, and therefore you think twice, if you have any sense, before bringing a case unless you have a very strong prospect of winning it, and unless what is involved in the case bears some sensible relation to the expense of bringing it."

Accordingly, the EAT held that the employee's conduct in failing to attend the hearing of his appeal was "unreasonable conduct in conducting the proceedings". He was ordered to pay towards the costs of the appeal incurred by the employers, who *had* attended the hearing.

Of course, the county court is not one of the superior courts in England and Wales; the small claims track is not concerned with employment appeals; the threshold to depart from fixed costs is not dependent on section 21(1) of the Employment Appeal Tribunal Rules 1976; and the threshold is not 'unreasonable conduct'.

Nonetheless, it exemplifies the following two submissions that may be made.

First, an award of costs *should* have the primary object of *minimising the financial detriment* to the successful party. In other words, *not* punishment. An award of costs must be *causally connected* to the finding that a party has behaved unreasonably.

Secondly, there is a public interest in safeguarding against irresponsible litigation, and therefore making *appropriate, justified* findings that a party has behaved unreasonably. There is no requirement for a causal connection. Finding that a party has behaved unreasonably is merely the peg on which costs hang.

ii. Statutory construction

The CPRs are secondary legislation (SI 1998/3132). When interpreting secondary legislation, where there is any real doubt as to its ordinary meaning, a dictionary may be consulted. In *R (on the Application of Mawbey & Ors) v Cornerstone Telecommunications Infrastructure Ltd* [2019] EWCA Civ 1016 at [22], Lord Justice Lindblom (with which Holroyde and King LJJ agreed) rightly said that, when interpreting legislation:

"If there were any real doubt as to the ordinary relevant meaning of the word, I can see no reason why one should not turn to dictionaries to dispel it. This is a well established technique of statutory construction, ..."

'Unreasonably' is defined in the Oxford English Dictionary (2nd edn, Clarendon Press, Oxford 1989) as follows:

1. In a manner at variance with reason; without due observance of reason or good judgment.
2. To an unreasonable extent; excessively, immoderately.

'Unreasonable' is defined as follows:

1. Not endowed with reason; irrational.
2. Not acting in accordance with reason or good sense; not reasonable in conduct, demands, expectations etc.
3. Not in accordance with reason; not based upon sound reason or good sense.
4. Going beyond what is reasonable or equitable; excessive in amount or degree.

c. Relevant circumstances

When deciding what order, if any, to make about costs, the court *must* have regard to the following, three circumstances (CPR 44.2(4)).

First, the conduct of *all* the parties. Secondly, whether a party has succeeded on *part* of its case, even if that party has not been wholly successful. Thirdly, any admissible offer to settle, which is drawn to the court's attention.

Conduct of the parties includes the following (CPR 44.2(5)).

First, conduct *before*, as well as *during* proceedings. In particular, the extent to which the parties have followed the Practice Direction – Pre-Action Conduct ("the Practice Direction"), or any relevant pre-action protocol (see appendix E).

Secondly, whether it was reasonable for a party to *raise*, *pursue*, or *contest* a particular allegation, or issue. Thirdly, the *manner* in which a party has pursued, or defended against a particular allegation or issue. Fourthly, whether a claimant who has succeeded, in whole or in part, *exaggerated* her claim.

i. Pre-action protocols & Practice Direction – Pre-Action Conduct

The pre-action protocols explain the conduct, and the steps that the court would *normally* expect parties to take before commencing proceedings (see chapter 4).

ii. Non-compliance

The court will take into account non-compliance *in substance* with the terms of the relevant pre-action protocol, or the Practice Direction. The court is not likely to be concerned with minor or technical infringements (CPR 44.3(5)(a)).

Where, on numerous occasions before proceedings are commenced, a defendant requests a key document (for example, an invoice) before agreeing to settle, failure to provide that invoice will likely amount to a failure to take reasonable and proportionate steps to achieve the objectives of the Practice Direction.

iii. Evidence

Ahead of the hearing, you can invite your *professional* client to write a very *short* witness statement, setting out any non-compliance. Where appropriate, relevant correspondence should be exhibited, and, if necessary, *very* briefly explained.

In principle, there is no requirement to file and serve a witness statement for the purpose of costs before a hearing. In practice, it often assists to do so, as it shows transparency, and provides the other party an opportunity to respond to your application.

Having had the benefit of notice, where no convincing response is forthcoming, this will only strengthen your application. In any event, the correspondence that you are relying on must be printed off, and there must be sufficient copies for the court, and the other party, so that, when making an application for costs on the basis that a party has behaved unreasonably, all court actors have the evidence.

iv. Issues raised, pursued or contested

A party will have failed to help the court to further the overriding objective where issues are unreasonably raised, pursued, or contested (CPR 1.3). Dealing with a case justly, and at proportionate cost, includes, so far as practicable, saving expense, ensuring that it is dealt with expeditiously and fairly, and allotting to it an appropriate share of the court's resources, while taking into account the need to allot resources to other cases (CPR 1.1(2)).

1. Abuse of process

At an extreme, claims and defences that are struck out as an abuse of process *should* attract a finding that a party has behaved unreasonably. Abusive statements of case reflect a *grievous* breach of the parties' duty to help the court to further the overriding objective to ensure that cases are dealt with fairly, and to ensure compliance with rules and practice directions.

2. Summary judgment

Going further down the spectrum, a claim or defence which is summarily judged to have no real prospect of success *may* also attract a finding that a party has behaved unreasonably in pursuing a statement of case that is unarguable. In this circumstance, the court is likely to require something more before in fact making a finding that a party has behaved unreasonably.

It will be remembered that, in *Dammermann* at paragraph 32, Lord Justice Longmore said that "it would be unfortunate if litigants were too easily deterred from using the Small Claims Track by the risk of being held to have behaved unreasonably and thus rendering themselves liable for costs".

There is a *qualitative* difference between an *abusive* statement of case, and one that has *no prospects of success*. A court may also find the fact that a party has been represented as constituting another, material difference.

a. Represented

Where a party is represented, the submission is likely to be stronger, as, in general, where there has been a failure to comply with a rule or a practice direction, it is not a good reason that that failure may be solely attributable to a legal representative (see chapter 17(h)(iii)(2)).

b. Unrepresented

Where a party is *un*represented, however, the court is more likely to grant permission to amend a statement of case, *if* it can be amended, so that there is a reasonable prospect of success. In any event, the court is likely to hesitate before finding that an *un*represented party, drafting her *own* statement of case, is culpable of behaving unreasonably, solely on the ground that her claim or defence has no real prospect of success.

3. Manner in which a case is pursued

In practice, there are two scenarios in which the *manner* that a party has conducted her case may amount to behaving unreasonably.

First, where there are *additional factors* surrounding failure to accept a *reasonable*, and *timely offer* to settle, in light of the *amount awarded* following judgment. Secondly, non-attendance of a party, or a key witness, where there has been no written notice, and no good reason for that absence.

a. Offers

Rejection of an offer in settlement will not, *of itself*, amount to behaving unreasonably, however, 'the court may take it into consideration when it is applying the unreasonableness test' (CPR 27.14(3)). There are three relevant circumstances surrounding an offer to settle.

First, who made it (claimant, or defendant). Secondly, when it was made (pre-action, early on in proceedings, or on the day of the final hearing). Thirdly, whether the offer was less than that awarded following judgment.

The fact that an offer was rejected is *not* sufficient for the court to find that the defendant has acted unreasonably. Add in three relevant circumstances, however, and it may be. For example, the *claimant* made the offer, *before* she issued the claim, for *half* of the amount that she was awarded following the final hearing.

In any event, before making a submission that a party has behaved unreasonably, identify *at least* one relevant circumstance, in addition to the mere fact that there has been a rejection of an offer to settle.

b. Non-attendance

Non-attendance is capable of forming the basis of a submission that the manner in which a party has pursued her claim or defence means that she had behaved unreasonably. Whether there has been written notice, the importance of the likely evidence that the witness is able to give, and whether there has been any other breach of a rule, practice direction, or court order, will often be determinative.

i. Party

Where a party does not attend, and does not give written notice, the court is entitled to find that that party has behaved unreasonably. If a claimant does not attend a final hearing, and does not give written notice, the court may strike out her claim. If a defendant does not attend a final hearing, the court may decide the claim on the basis of the claimant's evidence alone, provided that written notice was not given, and the claimant either attended the hearing, or gave written notice (see chapter 19(c)(i)).

ii. Witness

In principle, there is *no* requirement to serve a hearsay notice where a witness cannot attend trial (CPR 27.2(1)(c)). In practice, however, where that witness is *vital* to a party's case, the other party has *not been notified*, and *no (good) reason* has been given to justify the absence, the court is entitled to find that a party has behaved unreasonably.

In cases where liability is in dispute following a road traffic collision, for example, failure of a witness to attend may determine liability. The parties are under an obligation to help the court to further the overriding objective: to allot to the case an appropriate share of the court's resources, while taking into account the need to allot resources to other cases; and to enforce compliance with the rules, practice directions, and court orders.

Standard case management directions order the parties to notify the court of any reason that the time estimate for a case is likely to be substantially inaccurate. The submission is that, in this case, there is a breach of the rules, *and* a court order, justifying a finding that a party has behaved unreasonably.

4. Exaggeration

This is important for at least two reasons.

First, exaggerated claims will attract a higher *issue* fee, and a higher *hearing* fee. It is not *just*, and it is not *proportionate*, for a defendant to pay exaggerated court fees, regardless of whether or not the defence was successful. Secondly, exaggeration makes it difficult for a defendant to assess the true value of a claim, and to successfully settle the matter at an earlier stage.

Whilst there is no distinction in the rules between *in*tentional and *un*intentional exaggeration, the former *must* be considered in any assessment of costs. Further, to commence, pursue, and then to lose an exaggerated claim, without making any attempt to settle, "will often be conclusive" (*Painting v University of Oxford* [2005] EWCA Civ 161, [2005] Costs LR 394 at [22]).

5. Unnecessary applications

Unnecessary applications are incompatible with the overriding objective.

They do *not* assist the court to deal with the matter *justly* and *proportionately*, so far as is practicable. They do not: save expense; deal with the matter proportionately; ensure that the matter is dealt with expeditiously and fairly; and allot to it an appropriate share of the court's resources, taking into account the need to allot resources to other cases.

A written application, for example, to strike out a defence, which it was necessary to incur the cost of a skeleton argument to counter, and go on to defeat the claim entirely, provides one example. Of itself, this is unlikely to attract a finding that a party has behaved unreasonably. Coupled with *another* circumstance, however, it may tip the balance.

6. Communications

Any communication between a party and the court must be disclosed, and, if in writing, copied, to the other party, or her legal representative (CPRs 27.2(1)(h) and 39.8). This is regardless of whether the communication is on paper, or electronic. In short, *any* communication on a matter of *substance* or *procedure*.

There are three exceptions.

First, for *purely* routine, *un*contentious, and *administrative* correspondence. Secondly, where there is a *compelling* reason for not doing so, and this is *clearly stated* in the communication. Thirdly, where *authorised* by a rule or practice direction.

Correspondence to the court must state three matters.

First, that it *is* being copied to the other party. Secondly, the *identity* of the author. Thirdly, her *capacity* (for example, legal representative and solicitor). Unless the court otherwise directs, where there is a failure to do so, the court will return the correspondence to the sender, *without* being considered, but with a brief explanation as to why it is being returned.

Subject to hearing the parties, the court may impose sanctions, or exercise its general powers of case management (CPR 3) where there has been a failure to disclose, and to copy to the other party any communication on a matter of substance or procedure.

Failure to comply with the rules and practice directions when corresponding with the court, so as to deprive the other party of an opportunity to respond, amounts to "a serious procedural irregularity" (*National Westminster Bank Plc v Rushmer* [2010] EWHC 554 (Ch), [2010] 2 FLR 362 at [35]).

Where applicable, this is another factor that can be marshalled under a submission that a party has behaved unreasonably. The overriding objective includes ensuring that parties are on an equal footing. This cannot be achieved if one party ("A") is corresponding with the court on a matter of substance or procedure, without notice to the other party ("B"), so that B is not able to respond.

7. Opportunism

Where a party has opportunistically resisted an application that is bound to succeed, "heavy costs sanctions" should be imposed (*Denton & Ors v TH White Ltd & Ors* [2014] EWCA Civ 906, [2015] 1 All ER 880 at [43]). This is contrary to the duty of the parties to help the court to further the overriding objective, and frustrates the court exercising its duty actively to case-manage. In particular, to encourage the parties to cooperate (see chapter 3(a)).

d. Summary assessment

In principle, whenever a court makes an order about costs, which does not only provide for fixed costs to be paid, the court should deal with those costs at the *conclusion of the hearing*, unless there is a good reason not to do so (PD 44 at [9.2]). In practice, there will rarely (if ever) be a good reason not to do so in a claim that is allocated to the small claims track.

e. Statement of costs

Parties and their legal representatives must assist the court to make a summary assessment of costs. To do so, a written "statement of costs" should be prepared. In principle, it should follow as closely as possible Form N260. In practice, Form N260 is often used. In any event, it must be signed, either by the party, or that party's legal representatives (PD 44 at [9.5]).

i. Particulars

Separately, the following circumstances should be set out in a schedule (PD 44 at [9.5(2)]).

First, number of hours. Secondly, hourly rate. Thirdly, grade of fee earner. Fourthly, amount and nature of any disbursement (other than counsel's fee for appearing at the hearing). Fifthly, amount of legal representative's costs to be claimed for attending or appearing at the hearing. Sixthly, counsel's fees. Seventhly, any VAT to be claimed on these amounts.

1. Grade & number of hours

Be prepared to justify the number of hours that are claimed. Reasonableness will likely depend on two factors. First, *extent* and *complexity* of the procedural history. Secondly, grade of fee earner.

Of course, if there have been a number of previous applications, the number of hours worked on the case is likely to be higher than normal. In a straightforward claim for the cost of repairs following a road traffic collision, absent pre-final hearing applications, however, the court will expect a modest number of hours to have been invested in bringing the claim to a final hearing.

It is hard to justify a grade 'A' fee earner preparing a small claim. Where the claim, or the defence is abusive, there is a stronger argument that the issues are more complex, requiring a guiding, experienced hand. There is, of course, a limit. A lower grade of fee earner will usually justify a larger number of hours, and vice versa.

2. Rate

Solicitors' guideline hourly rates can be found online (www.gov.uk/guidance/solicitors-guideline-hourly-rates). From 2010, they are as follows:

Pay band	Fee earner	London grade			National grade		
		1	2	3	1	2	3
A	Solicitors & legal executives with over eight years' experience	£409	£317	£229 to £267	£217	£201	£201
B	Solicitors & legal executives with over four years' experience	£296	£242	£172 to £229	£192	£177	£177
C	Other solicitors or legal executives & fee earners of equivalent experience	£226	£196	£165	£161	£146	£146
D	Trainee solicitors, paralegals & other fee earners	£138	£126	£121	£118	£111	£111

a. London

Grade 1 encompasses the City of London EC1-EC4. Grade 2 encompasses Central London W1, WC1, WC2, and SW1. Grade 3 encompasses all other, outer London postcodes.

b. National

Grade 1 encompasses: Aldershot, Farnham, Bournemouth (including Poole); Birmingham Inner; Bristol; Cambridge City, Harlow; Canterbury, Maidstone, Medway, Tunbridge Wells; Cardiff (Inner); Chelmsford South, Essex, East Suffolk; Fareham, Winchester; Hampshire, Dorset, Wiltshire, Isle of Wight; Kingston, Guildford, Reigate, Epsom; Leeds Inner (within two kilometres of City Art Gallery); Lewes; Liverpool, Birkenhead; Manchester Central; Newcastle (City Centre) (within 2 metres of St Nicholas Cathedral); Norwich City; Nottingham City; Oxford, Thames Valley; Southampton, Portsmouth; Swindon, Basingstoke; and Watford.

Grade 2 encompasses: Bath, Cheltenham, Gloucester, Taunton, Yeovil; Bury; Chelmsford North, Cambridge County, Peterborough, Bury St Edmunds, Norfolk, Lowestoft; Chester; North Wales; Coventry, Rugby, Nuneaton, Stratford, Warwick; Exeter, Plymouth; Hull (City) Leeds Outer, Wakefield, Pontefract; Leigh; Lincoln; Luton, Bedford, St Albans, Hitchin, Hertford; Manchester Outer, Oldham, Bolton, Tameside; Newcastle (other than City Centre); Nottingham, Derbyshire; Sheffield, Doncaster, South Yorkshire; Southport; St Helens; Stockport, Altrincham, Salford; Swansea, Newport, Cardiff Outer; Wigan; Wolverhampton, Walsall, Dudley, Stourbridge; and York, Harrogate.

Grade 3 encompasses: Birmingham Outer; Bradford, Dewsbury, Halifax, Huddersfield, Keighley, Skipton; Cumbria; Devon, Cornwall; Grimsby, Skegness; Hull Outer; Kidderminster; Northampton, Leicester; Preston, Lancaster, Blackpool, Chorley, Accrington, Burnley, Blackburn, Rawenstall, Nelson; Scarborough, Ripon; Stafford, Stoke,

Tamworth; Teesside; Worcester, Hereford, Evesham, Redditch; Shrewsbury, Telford, Ludlow, Oswestry; and South and West Wales.

ii. Notice

The statement of costs must be filed at court, and copies must be served on the other party as soon as possible, and, in any event, not less than 24 hours before the time fixed for the hearing.

Without reasonable excuse, failure to do so will be taken into account when deciding what order to make about costs (PD 44 at [9.6]).

It is prudent to take a spare hard copy of the statement of costs to the hearing, as well as the correspondence, evidencing filing, and service, in case there is a dispute over the same.

iii. Absence

Where there is no statement of costs, practice managers, or, failing that, professional clients should be able to confirm counsel's fee. The court is often invited to award that sum, together with any applicable VAT, so as to deal with the matter of costs swiftly, and save the expense of a further hearing.

25. Appeals

Where there is a reasonable prospect of successfully appealing an order, or a judgment, advise that this is the case, and, if instructed, ask for permission to appeal. Although you must only make a *written* application for permission to appeal on *express* instructions, it is part of your *implied* instructions to make an *oral* application for permission to appeal where appropriate.

a. Court

The "appeal court" is the court to which an appeal must be made. The "lower court" is the court from whose decision an appeal is brought (CPR 52.1(3)(b) and (c)).

For a first appeal, the appeal court from a district judge is the circuit judge at the same county court. In the rare circumstance that a circuit judge heard the claim, the appeal court is a single judge of the High Court. These are the correct appeal courts, whether the decision was interim, or final. For a second appeal, the appeal court is the Court of Appeal (PD 52A at [3.4], [3.5], and Table 1).

b. Centre

Appeals must be brought in the appropriate "appeal centre". All other notices, such as the respondent's notice, must also be filed at that appeal centre. The venue for an appeal will be determined by the designated civil judge, which may be different from the appeal centre (PD 52B at [2.2] and Table A).

c. Permission

Permission is needed to appeal, for which there are two tests.

One for first appeals. The other for second appeals. An oral, or a written application can be made, requiring four documents, grounds of appeal, and an appeal bundle.

Application can also be made for a stay of the lower court's order, and an extension of time in which to file an appellant's notice.

i. Need

Any party wishing to appeal requires permission (CPR 52.3(1)). This includes where a party wishes to appeal against an order made without a hearing, or in that party's absence in accordance with her request (PD 27 at [8.2]).

In principle, an application for permission to appeal may be made to the *lower* court that made the decision being appealed (CPR 52.3(2)). In practice, this court often refuses, so that an application must be made to the *appeal* court (CPR 52.3(3)).

ii. Test

The test for permission to appeal depends on whether it is a *first* or *second* appeal.

1. First appeal

Permission *may* only be given for a first appeal where one of the following two criteria applies (CPR 52.6(1)).

First, the court considers that the appeal would have a *real prospect of success*. Secondly, there is some other, *compelling* reason for the appeal to be heard.

Permission is *not* granted as of right, even where the test is satisfied. The court has a *discretion*, as is clear from the word "may".

In practice, the first limb of the test is most frequently relied upon. In the words of Lord Justice Peter Jackson in *R (A Child)* [2019] EWCA Civ 895 at [31] (with which Lord Justice Baker agreed), "there must be a realistic, as opposed to a fanciful, prospect of success. There is no requirement that success should be probable, or more likely than not."

2. Second appeal

The Court of Appeal *will not* give permission for a second appeal, unless it considers that one of the following two criteria are satisfied (CPR 52.7(2)).

First, the appeal would have a real prospect of success *and raise an important point of principle or practice*. Secondly, there is some other, compelling reason *for the Court of Appeal* to hear it.

From a decision of the county court, which was itself made on appeal, only the Court of Appeal can give permission for a second appeal (CPR 52.7(1)). Permission is *not* granted as of right, *even* where the test is satisfied.

Again, in practice, the first limb of the test is most frequently relied on.

The *first* part of the *first* limb of the second appeal test is the same as the *first* limb of the *first* appeal test. The *second* part of the *first* limb – that is, an important point of practice or principle is raised – means one "that has not yet been established". This has recently been confirmed by Lord Justice McCombe (with whom) Lord Justice Richard agreed) in *BS (Congo) & Ors v Secretary of State for the Home Department* [2015] EWCA Civ 639 at [17].

iii. Oral application

After judgment and costs, an oral application for permission to appeal may be made.

Reasons for the application should be *clearly*, but *concisely* set out. It is part of your implied instructions to make an oral application for permission to appeal where appropriate. If you fail to do so, an opportunity to gain permission, *without incurring the cost of a written application*, will have been lost.

No fee is required to make an oral application.

iv. Appellant's notice

Where permission is sought from the appeal court, it must be in the form of an "appellant's notice". This is Form N164 (PDs 27 at [8A] and 52B at [4.1]). Guidance on completing an appellant's notice is available in Form N161A.

As a general rule, it must be filed at the appeal court within 21 days after the date of the decision of the lower court. The period may be longer, or shorter, as ordered by the lower court. The CPRs and practice directions regarding time limits apply (PD 52D). Unless the appeal court orders otherwise, an appellant's notice must be served on each respondent as soon as practicable, and, in any event, no later than seven days after it is filed.

1. Fee

An appellant's notice must be accompanied by the fee of £120, fee remission application, or certificate (PD 52B at [4.1] and chapter 23(b) (iv)).

2. Documents

There are four documents that must be filed with the appellant's notice (52B at [4.2]).

First, three copies of the appellant's notice, and one additional copy for each respondent. Secondly, a copy of the sealed order under appeal. Thirdly, where an application was made to the lower court for permission to appeal, a copy of any order granting or refusing permission to appeal, together with a copy of the reasons, if any, for allowing, or refusing permission to appeal. Fourthly, grounds of appeal.

3. Grounds

The grounds of appeal must be set out on a *separate* sheet and *attached* to the appellant's notice. They must set out one of the following two grounds (CPR 52.21(3)).

First, the decision of the lower court was *wrong*. Secondly, it was unjust because of a serious *procedural* or other *irregularity* in proceedings.

Either way, it must be in simple language, clear and concise.

4. Transcript

There is no *requirement* to obtain, file, or serve, a transcript of the judgment of the lower court, or other record of reasons (PD 52B at [6.2]). Although, it *may* assist the appeal court, depending on the grounds of appeal.

v. Respondent's notice

A respondent *may* file and serve a "respondent's notice". This is Form N162. Guidance for completing it is available in Form N162A.

A respondent *must* file a respondent notice in two circumstances (CPR 52.13(2)).

First, where permission to appeal is sought from the *appeal* court by the *respondent* herself. Secondly, the respondent wishes to ask the appeal court to uphold the decision of the lower court for reasons *different* from, or *additional* to, those given by the lower court.

1. Permission

Where permission is sought from the appeal court, it *must* be in the respondent's notice. It must be filed within such period as directed by the lower court, or, 14 days after the "relevant date". The latter depends on which of the following circumstances apply.

Where *permission* to appeal was *granted* by the *lower* court, or permission to appeal is *not* required, the relevant date is when the respondent is *served* with the appellant's notice. When the *respondent* is served with notification that the *appeal* court has *given* the appellant permission to appeal, this is the relevant date. When the *respondent* is served with notification that the *application* for permission to appeal and the *appeal* itself are to be heard together, this is the relevant date.

2. Service

Unless otherwise ordered by the appeal court, the respondent's notice must be served on the appellant, and any other respondent, as soon as practicable, and, in any event, no later than seven days after it is filed.

d. Skeleton arguments

Skeleton arguments should *not* be filed and served in an appeal as a matter of course.

They should be used only where they are *justified* on the basis of the *complexity* of the issues of fact or law in the appeal, or they would otherwise assist the court in respects that are *not readily apparent from the papers* in the appeal (PD 52B at [8.3]).

Remember that, in general, costs of a successful appeal will *not* be awarded (see below).

e. Appeal bundle

As soon as practicable, but in any event, within 25 days of filing the appellant's notice, the appellant must file an appeal bundle. It must contain *only* those documents relevant to the appeal, subject to any order made by the court. An appeal bundle must be *paginated* and *indexed* (PD 52B at [6.3]).

i. Relevant

There are six documents that are "relevant" to an appeal (PD 52B at [6.4(1)]).

First, the appellant's notice. Secondly, any respondent's notice. Thirdly, any skeleton argument. Fourthly, the order under appeal. Fifthly, the order of the lower court, granting or refusing permission to appeal, together with a copy of the judge's reasons (if any). Sixthly, a copy of any order allocating the case to the small claims track.

Any relevant document, obtained, or created after the appeal bundle has been filed, should be added to the appeal bundle as soon as practicable. In any event, no less than seven days before the hearing of the appeal, or any application (PD 52B at [6.6]).

ii. May be relevant

Where relevant, the following seven documents *should* also be included (PD 52B at [6.4(2)]).

First, statements of case. Secondly, application notices. Thirdly, other orders made in the case. Fourthly, chronology of relevant events. Fifthly, witness statements made in support of any application made in the appellant's notice. Sixthly, any other witness statements. Seventhly, any other documents, which any party considers would assist the appeal court.

iii. Service

There are three rules prescribing when the appeal bundle must be served on each respondent (PD 52B at [6.5]).

First, where *permission* to appeal was *granted* by the *lower* court, service must be at the same time as *filing* the appeal bundle. Secondly, where the *appeal* court has *granted* permission to appeal, *as soon as practicable* after notification, and, in any event, *within 14 days* of the grant of permission. Thirdly, where the *appeal* court directs that the *application* for permission to appeal will be heard on the *same* occasion as the *appeal*, *as soon as practicable*, and, in any event, *within 14 days* after notification of the hearing date.

iv. Respondent's documents

Where a respondent considers that relevant documents have been omitted, she may file and serve on all parties a "respondent's supplemental appeal bundle". It should contain copies of relevant documents that have been *omitted* from the appeal bundle. It must be filed and served as soon as practicable, and, in any event, no less than seven days before the hearing (PD 52B at 8.2).

f. Applications

Applications should be made to the *lower* court, but, where the time limit for filing an appellant's notice has expired, they should be made to the *appeal* court.

i. Stay

An application can be made in the appeal for a *stay* of the order of the lower court. If so, it should be included within the appellant's notice (PD 52B at [4.3]).

ii. Extension

Application can be made in the appeal for an extension of time in which to file an appellant's notice. It must be made at the same time as the appellant applies to the lower court for permission to appeal (PD 52B at [3.1]). Where the time limit for filing an appellant's notice has expired, however, the appellant must include an application within the appellant's notice (PD 52B at [3.2] and [4.3]).

It must state two particulars (PD 52B at [3.2]). First, the *reason* for the delay. Secondly, the *steps that have been taken*, prior to making the application.

The court *may* make an order granting or refusing an extension of time. It may be with or without a hearing. If it is without a hearing, any party seeking to set aside or vary the order may apply for a hearing, within 14 days of service of the order (PD 52B at [3.3]).

g. Determination

Applications, including an application for permission to appeal, may be determined with or without a hearing (PD 52B at [7.1]).

Where permission to appeal is refused without a hearing, the party may *request* that the application is reconsidered at a hearing. Where the court determines any other application without a hearing, any party affected by that determination may *apply* to have the order set aside or varied.

In any event, the following three conditions apply (PD 52B at [7.4]).

First, the request or application must be made *within seven days* of service of the notification of the determination upon the party making the application. Secondly, a copy of the request or application must be served on *all other parties* at the *same* time. Thirdly, the court will give directions for the determination of the application.

Where an appeal is allowed, the appeal court will, wherever possible, dispose of the case at the *same* time, *without* ordering that there is a further hearing in the lower court. The court may do so without hearing further evidence (PD 27 at [8.3]).

h. Costs

The costs regime for cases allocated to the small claims track applies to the costs of an appeal (*Akhtar v Boland (Costs)* [2014] EWCA Civ 943, [2014] CP Rep 41 at [7]).

26. Attendance notes

An attendance note ("a note") can be very condensed, or more complete, containing close to a word-for-word alternative to a transcript. In any event, the practice of writing a couple of sentences on a back sheet is (I am told) dying out. There are a number of good reasons for this (see below).

There are no set rules for notes, albeit that there are pieces of information which any note should strive to contain, such as the name of the court, judge, legal representative (if there is one), and the terms of any order. In a competitive legal market, professional clients may be more inclined to provide repeat instructions to counsel for which there is tangible, written evidence of an ability to engender the trust and confidence of *their* client, deliver sound legal submissions, which it is clear have had the desired impact looking at the reasoning in the judgment.

a. Utility

Notes are helpful. For counsel, those instructing, and the party that they represent. Albeit in different ways, and for different reasons.

i. Counsel

For counsel, it offers an opportunity to make a clear, contemporary, and comprehensive note of what has been said, complete with any relevant context. For example, the time that a conference started, that the witness had an opportunity to read an unmarked copy of her statement, and that she confirmed the truth of it, without any suggested amendments. During cross-examination, the witness may admit that, for example, she was not wearing a seat belt at the moment of collision, yet her written evidence confirms the contrary.

The note may provide that the witness did not take the opportunity in conference to correct it. If this inconsistency is cited in the judgment as a reason that the credibility of this witness was undermined, then, the note may provide counsel with reassurance that they gave the witness an opportunity to re-read the statement, and amend it, ahead of the final hearing. If there is any dispute as to what was said in that conference, perhaps days, months, or even years later, a detailed note goes some way to be able to provide an answer.

ii. Professional client

For a professional client, a note should have five pieces of information.

First, what points were successful, and the reasons why. Secondly, what points were not successful, and the reasons why. Thirdly, the total amount of the judgment sum. Fourthly, a breakdown of the amounts awarded for each head of loss. Fifthly, any payment terms that were ordered, such as payment within 21 (as opposed to 14) days.

If your lay client asks your professional client what was discussed in conference, what oral evidence was given, and what were the reasons for judgment against them, your professional client is able to respond, promptly, in detail, and with confidence. This is another reason that your note should be received by your *professional* client promptly, so that they are able to field questions from *their* client, as and when they are asked after a hearing. A professional client will not appreciate being kept in the dark, as this may compromise *their* relationship with *their* client, due to their inability to answer questions, advise on next steps, and thereby retain the trust and confidence of *their* client.

iii. Lay client

For a party, they may wish to confirm, for example, the reasoning in the judgment as to why they were held to be an unreliable historian of events. A comprehensive note of the judgment will enable them to do so, promptly, through speaking over the telephone with your professional client. It will also enable a party to instruct counsel to advise whether or not there are prospects of successfully appealing, without having to wait, and to incur the cost of a transcript.

Remember that your lay client may request to see your note of the hearing. This may inform whether or not you wish to include, for example: your mobile telephone; and a warts and all view of the reasonableness, or otherwise, of your lay client as a person, their credibility, and their witness. This is not code to conceal; it is a caution to take a *professional* note.

b. Fundamentals

At the top of the note, it is helpful to set out the following nine details.

First, the names of the parties as they appear on the statements of case. Secondly, the claim number. Thirdly, the name of the court. Fourthly, the number of the courtroom. Fifthly, the title, and the name of the judge. Sixthly, the date of the hearing.

Seventhly, the type of hearing (application or final). Eighthly, the title, surname, and status (counsel or solicitor) of the advocate who represents the other party. Ninthly, the contact details of your professional client, including her name, firm, and email address.

c. Outcome

The outcome of the application or final hearing should be on the first page, so that it is clear.

d. Correspondence

Any correspondence, with your professional client, instructions taken in conference from your lay client, or issues raised by the other party can be noted. This is helpful, especially where, for example, an offer to settle is made. It may be useful to have a note of the terms of that offer after the hearing, when the issue of costs is decided, and for your professional client to quantify future, similar cases.

i. Professional client

For counsel, it may be helpful to record that a key document, such as an invoice, has been requested from a professional client *ahead* of the hearing, in *writing*, via email; and followed up with a *telephone* conversation. If the head of loss to which that invoice relates is then dismissed, there is evidence that counsel has discharged her duty to *foresee* obvious problems, and *promptly* attempt to resolve them.

The terms of any offer to settle (including provision for costs) should also be recorded, as well as the time that it was made, and who made it. When you relayed that offer to your professional client, your advice as to whether or not it is in your client's interests to accept that offer, and your instructions from your professional client, should both be noted.

If an offer to settle is made, and you advise your professional client that, the *best* alternative to a settlement out of court is judgment for the same, or even *less* than that offer, and your client does not beat that offer after a final hearing, the question *why* that offer was not accepted may reasonably arise. If you are able to set out the above, and that you did not have authority to accept that offer, despite receipt of your advice, counsel has discharged their professional duty.

ii. Lay client

Instructions taken in conference should be noted. What time the conference started, when the witness read an unmarked copy of her statement, and confirmed the contents of that statement, without suggesting amendments, are useful to note. Of course, if the witness changes a material part of her written evidence under cross-examination, thereby undermining her credibility, so that the case that you are instructed to present is dismissed, counsel cannot be criticised.

The *exact* words of any suggested amendment should also be noted, and the *paragraph* of the written statement to which those words relate. It is often helpful for a witness to read the other party's statement(s), and to take a note of what that witness says in *response* to material evidence that conflicts with your party's case. This can be particularly helpful when cross-examining, and, generally, to understand your party's case.

iii. Other party

When you speak to the other party before the hearing, summarise the material points that arose out of that discussion. As well as offers to settle, the issues that are in dispute, and any procedural issues – such as an allegation that a document has not been served – are helpful to note for three reasons.

First, to have at your fingertips during the hearing, especially if you are representing the claimant, and summarising the issues in dispute. Secondly, so that you can speak to your professional client, relay the same *accurately*, and take *precise* instructions. Thirdly, so that your professional client can understand the other party's position *ahead* of the hearing, and compare that to the judgment, *after* the hearing.

e. Tactical & strategic decisions

Any *tactical* or *strategic* decision before a hearing should be noted.

For example, the defendant has to make an application for relief from sanctions for failure to serve a key document, such as an invoice. The claimant wishes to rely on video footage of the collision that has not been filed or served until the day of the final hearing. On instructions, and on receipt of your advice, the decision is taken not to resist the claimant relying on this video, so as to assist the defendant's application for relief from sanctions. If instructions were taken over the telephone, the time of that call, and the person giving instructions may be noted.

The video may feature heavily in the reasoning of the court in coming to judgment *against the party that you represent.* Succinctly summarising the circumstances in which this strategic decision was made can be helpful for counsel, those instructing, and the lay client. This is because, if it is asked why reliance on the video was not resisted, say, a week after the final hearing, when memories have faded, and oral recollections appear less credible, the answer is in a written, contemporaneous note.

f. Additional instructions

Any additional instructions to those in the brief to counsel, whether obtained over the telephone, or via email, should be noted here. This is so that, in days, months, or years to come, if there is a question as to why something was, or was not submitted, agreed, or conceded, there is a contemporaneous note recording the reason. You may have deleted the email instructing you not to pursue a counterclaim, for example, in accordance with your privacy policy.

g. During hearing

Some make an accurate, word-for-word note of the hearing. Others summarise. Either way, submissions, oral evidence, judgment, and the terms of the order are useful to note.

i. Shorthand

The time that the hearing was called on is helpful to note, in case of an appeal, where a transcript of the hearing may be requested.

Counsel for the claimant, Ms Smith, may be shortened to "S". Whenever Ms Smith addresses the court, a note can be made using shorthand. For example: 'S: this is a case for credit hire, where need, enforceability, impecuniosity, period, and rate, are the issues that are in dispute.' The judge can be shortened to "J".

ii. Evidence

The time that a witness is called can be noted, again, in case of an appeal, and a transcript is requested. The oral evidence given by a witness should be noted carefully. Instead of typing out the question, and the answer, separately, you can combine the two.

Take the question: "You could have used public transport?" And the answer: "I have a disabled mother, who I often take to the hospital." They can be combined to: "I could not use public transport as I have a disabled mother, who I often take to the hospital."

If a witness makes a concession in your cross-examination, and you wish to refer to it in your closing submissions, you can **embolden** it, so that it stands out, and it is easily found. It is more persuasive to use the *actual words* used by a witness, rather than paraphrase. If your witness says something on which you wish to re-examine, again, you can embolden it, so that you can quickly navigate to it.

Sometimes, the judge will comment on a piece of evidence, submission, or the conduct of a party. If it assists your case, again, it can be emboldened, for ease of reference. Then, it can be incorporated into your closing submissions, or application for costs on the basis that a party has behaved unreasonably, or perhaps, both. If it is something that you would like to address, again, emboldening it will enable you to find it, and to rely on it at the appropriate time.

iii. Submissions

Take a note of the other party's closing submissions for three reasons.

First, if there is anything that you *need* to address, this will remind you to address it. Secondly, if a *concession* is made, you can rely on it in *your* closing submissions. Thirdly, when advising on prospects of successfully appealing, it can be helpful to know how the other party put their case in closing.

iv. Judgment

As close to a word-for-word note of the judgment as possible is helpful for four reasons.

First, to explain to your lay client why, for example, her case was dismissed, she was not awarded what she claimed, or the reasons that the judge found that the credibility of a witness was compromised. Secondly, to advise on prospects of successfully appealing, or of resisting an appeal. Where there may be prospects of appeal, the relevant sentence, paragraph, or passage can be emboldened, so that it stands out from the rest of the judgment.

Thirdly, so that both you, and your professional client have *tangible* evidence of what submissions succeeded, failed, and were of no consequence to the outcome. This is so that, in future cases, *you* can hone your submissions, your *professional* client can perfect statements of case, and thereby, both fulfil professional duties to further *clients'* best interests, and helping the *court* to further the overriding objective.

Fourthly, if the order is incompatible with the judgment, there may have been an error. If so, this may be corrected by the slip rule. Without an accurate note of the judgment, you are in a weaker position to advise on whether or not there has been an error, and what the order *should* read, so that it accurately reflects the judgment.

v. Order

The terms of the order are *fundamental*. They should be set out on the first page.

You may also wish to copy and paste the same into the email to your professional client, attaching the note, for two reasons. First, for the convenience of your *professional* client. Secondly, so that your *practice manager*, who is unlikely to open your note, will see whether or not your client has been successful. As a pupil, this may be especially important.

h. Next steps

If the hearing was an application, after which the court made case management directions, this is a good place to make a note of the same. Any summary advice on next steps should be included here. Usually, there is no reason that it should be longer than, say, a paragraph.

i. Travel expenses

It is helpful to set out any travel expenses for two reasons. Of course, train tickets should still be retained for tax purposes; and a record of your journeys using a registered Oyster card can be downloaded as a pdf, and then saved for your accountant.

First, your practice manager may have agreed that they should be billed, in addition to the brief fee, especially where the court is some distance from your chambers. Secondly, when working out your expenses for tax purposes, your notes provide a convenient record. This is a failsafe if you are not as fastidious in going through your expenses every month or so, so that, when you *do* come around to it, you are able to recall your travel expenses *in detail*.

j. Contact details

At the bottom of a note, the name of your practice manager, their contact details, and your professional address should be set out, should your professional client wish to contact you. Remember that your lay client may ask to see the note, so bear this in mind if you give your mobile telephone number.

k. Telephone

After the hearing, consider telephoning your professional client for two reasons.

First, to relay the result *promptly*, so that your *professional* client is able to answer questions, should the *lay* client telephone. You may take some time proofreading your note. Secondly, this is another opportunity to build rapport with a professional client, who may be based at the other end of the country, so that your opportunities to speak, and market your practice, are limited.

l. Email

Once completed, email your note to your professional client, ideally on the same day as the hearing, but, in any event, within 24 hours. Professional clients choose repeatedly to instruct counsel who send notes promptly. It is a good idea to copy your practice manager into this email, for three reasons.

First, your practice manager will know that the case can be billed. Secondly, if there will be a further (final) hearing, but, due to another professional commitment, you are *un*able to attend, your practice manager is able to forward on the note to counsel who *will* attend. Thirdly, if your professional client contacts your practice manager to say that they have not received your note, your practice manager can forward on your note, without having to revert to you.

27. Tools

Just as a plumber has a number of readily identifiable, frequently used tools of the trade, there are a number of items that often come in useful to a junior advocate in a claim that has been allocated to the small claims track. A smart phone, laptop, and access to online, electronic legal resources are invaluable to be able to correspond, type up attendance notes, orders, and look up an authority that has arisen just before, during, or after a hearing.

a. Smart phone

Most carry a mobile telephone. The majority of these will be "smart phones".

A *mobile telephone* is necessary to communicate with your professional client.

To relay that a witness is late, for example, and to receive instructions that the good reason for this is that that witness has been admitted to an accident and emergency hospital department. It is also necessary to communicate with your practice manager, for example, to relay that your train has been delayed, or to receive the notification that, in fact, the hearing has been vacated. Offers to settle must be relayed to those instructing promptly, so that instructions can be taken as to whether that offer is acceptable, and to receive the terms of a last-minute counter-offer.

A *smart phone* is helpful for three reasons.

First, to check train times, buy train tickets, and plan your route to and from court, using the full range of public transport options, including tube, train, and bus. Secondly, to use online navigation software, so as to locate the county court when you arrive at a station. Thirdly, so that you can tether your smart phone to your laptop, so that you can access the internet.

b. Laptop

Both a portable computer, and the software necessary to utilise it efficiently, are *invaluable*. Remember to take a laptop charger, too, especially when your case is on an unassigned list, so as to mitigate against the risk of running out of battery.

i. Hardware

A laptop is invaluable for three reasons.

First, so that you have an electronic copy of the papers, should you have to hand a spare, hard copy to the court, or use it as a witness bundle. Secondly, so that you can take an accurate note of the hearing, swiftly proofread that note, and promptly email it to those instructing. Thirdly, so that, tethered to your smart phone, you can send and receive emails, access online, electronic legal resources, and log into your online diary (if you have one).

ii. Software

Software should be updated regularly so that your laptop does not crash, or you otherwise lose the ability to work on, save, and access documents, *temporarily*, inside or outside of court, or even *permanently*. In the case of the latter, unless you have another laptop, your ability to practise will be *severely* restricted for days, if not a week or so.

c. Online resources

Access to an electronic version of a professional text will save you from carrying a hard copy to and from court, day in, day out, week in, week out. There are professional texts that can be saved onto an electronic device. Online access is preferable, however, for two reasons.

First, the *number* of professional texts, and authorities that you can access online, and the corresponding *impracticality* of taking hard copies of the same to court, or of saving electronic copies to your electronic device. Secondly, when accessed, you can be confident that you are reading a version that is likely to be more up to date than one that has been printed, or one that has been saved onto your device, in either case, *some time ago*.

Not infrequently, you may recall an authority that assists your case, but, because the point that that authority goes to has only been raised during submissions, you have not printed hard copies for the court and the other party. If you have online access to an electronic database, you can find the name, citation, and paragraph of that authority, explain the reason that you have not provided hard copies in advance of the hearing, and serve the best interests of your client, and help the court to deal with the matter justly and proportionately, without the need for an adjournment, or even an appeal.

d. Notepad

There are two reasons to carry a notepad and a black, ball-point pen.

First, in case your laptop crashes, or is otherwise unworkable. Secondly, from time-to-time, the court may insist that a hard copy of an order is handed to an usher, rather than an electronic version is sent to the court, attached to an email. For this reason, it is a good idea to carry an A4, lined notepad.

Once back in chambers, this page may be scanned, emailed to you, and sent to your professional client, or just stored on your external, encrypted hard drive. In either case, the hard copy can be disposed of confidentially, assisting your practice to become paperless, and thereby furthering the objectives of data protection, and privacy policies (see below).

Writing should be in black ink, and text should be in capital letters, so that, when scanned, and photocopied, it remains legible. Although there are aesthetic benefits to a fountain pen, it can pay dividends to carry a black ball-point pen, just in case.

e. Disk drive

Not infrequently, your professional client will include a disk in your instructions. That disk may store a video, captured by a dashboard camera, showing the weather conditions, road layout, location, and perhaps even the mechanism of a collision. If so, it may assist, or undermine the case that you are instructed to present.

If it assists, it is in your client's interests to rely on it. If it undermines your case, it is likely that the other party will seek to rely on it. If it cannot be played, there is a risk that the case will be adjourned, and, if your client goes on to lose the case, she will have incurred time and cost through *your* failure to be able to play the video.

Disk drives no longer come as standard in many new, slimline laptops. If your laptop does not have an *in*-built disk drive, consider purchasing an *external* one. The chances are that you will, at one stage, view this as a necessary investment.

f. Tablet

If there is a video showing a road traffic collision, you may need to play it, so that the *court*, and the *witness* can see it. In the likely event that you are required to cross-examine on it, it is not possible to play the video on your laptop, so that the *witness* and the *judge* can see it, and *you* are able to simultaneously take a note of that witness' answers on your laptop. Accordingly, a separate electronic device, such as a tablet, solves this problem.

g. The Highway Code

Where liability is in dispute, *The Highway Code* is essential for final hearings following a road traffic collision. It is the starting point for identifying the standard of care that is expected of a reasonable driver (see chapter 20(e)).

h. Judicial College Guidelines

Where there is a claim for personal injury, the *Judicial College Guidelines for the Assessment of General Damages in Personal Injury Cases* (15th edn, OUP 2019) is essential (see chapter 20(f)).

i. Props

In cases arising from a road traffic collision, some may find toy or model cars useful for conferences, and even final hearings. The reasons include that a witness can demonstrate the mechanism of collision, point of impact, and where the corresponding damage is on both vehicles. Alternatively, two other items (such as highlighters) can be used.

j. External encrypted vault

Electronic devices should be *sanitised promptly* of confidential material, in accordance with your data protection, and privacy policies. Your chambers should have a policy. If you are not familiar with it, there should be online access, or, failing that, you should be able to request a copy.

Once a case is concluded, there is no good reason to retain confidential material relating to it on a *portable* electronic device, that you transport between your home, chambers, and court, often via public transport.

To comply with data protection and privacy laws, external hard drives containing confidential material *must* be encrypted. There are two forms of encryption: *hard* and *soft*. In general, hardware encryption is preferable. That is, with a keypad that requires a *numerical code* to be entered before the hard drive will be recognised, files can be accessed, or transferred onto another electronic device.

At least one, *encrypted*, external hard drive is *vital* to good practice management.

One can be kept under lock and key in chambers. Another can be kept at another location, such as your home, again, under lock and key. The former should be periodically updated onto the latter, which then functions as a secure "vault", so as to guard against the worst-case scenario, for example, a fire at chambers.

28. Dress

'Court dress: Revised Guidance from the Chairman of the Bar Council' (2 June 2009) is the guidance for counsel, but it does *not* prescribe dress for *applications* or *final hearings* before *(deputy) district judges*.

For *appeals* from applications, however, it provides that counsel must wear business suits.

In practice, dark-coloured business suits, and black, leather-looking shoes are worn in applications and final hearings of claims that are allocated to the small claims track. Men wear neckties. Court dress must be worn for *appeals from final hearings*, that is, wigs, gowns, wing collars and bands, or collarettes.

29. Ethics

Practising barristers and solicitors are bound by their respective codes of conduct. They are taken as read for the purposes of this guide. There is some *practical* guidance below, however, in the context of claims that are allocated to the small claims track.

a. Confidants

Prepare in advance of an ethical issue. It is helpful, and comforting, to store the numbers, and the email addresses of several *appropriately* experienced, reliable, and trustworthy colleagues. Depending on the scenario, Queen's Counsel is unlikely to be the appropriate level of experience needed to advise on an ethical question relating to a claim that is allocated to the small claims track.

Ideally, they should not be so senior that they are likely to be unfamiliar with claims that are allocated to the small claims track. You should be confident that, if they can, they will answer your call, or otherwise revert to you as soon as practicable. You should be able to confide in them, as many advocates in claims that are allocated to the small claims track are pupils, and other junior advocates, who will be grateful that their questions are not relayed back to more senior colleagues, without permission.

Often, a telephone call can be the quickest means of relaying an issue, receiving guidance, and reassurance. If all of the telephone numbers that you have are engaged, or you cannot otherwise speak to someone, send an email. If time is of the essence, another option is to speak to your practice manager, enquire whether any of your colleagues are available, and request to be put through to the one who is most appropriate.

b. Ethical Enquiries Services

If it is not possible to speak to a colleague, the Bar Council's Ethical Enquiries Service is confidential. It provides assistance to counsel *to identify*, *interpret*, and *comply with* their professional obligations. Monday to Friday, from 09:15 to 17:15, this service is available by calling 020 7611 1207.

30. Etiquette

Etiquette goes hand in hand with professional ethics. A core duty of counsel is not to behave in a way that is likely to diminish trust and confidence that the public place in you, and generally, in the profession. Failure to show respect and courtesy to court actors, for example, through following the appropriate etiquette, may breach this duty.

a. Outside court

Punctual arrival at court, appropriate use of the advocates' room, disposal of confidential documents, and correspondence all follow a customary code of polite, professional behaviour.

i. Punctuality

Like any other professional, you should plan to arrive in the right *place*, at the right *time*, with the right *tools*, and the right *attitude*. Public transport may be delayed, listings can go awry, and personal circumstances can conspire against you. The ethical question is often not *whether or not* you are late, but the *reason* why, and what you have done to *mitigate* the effects of it.

If there is a reasonable prospect that you will be late, speak to your practice manager, your professional client, and *ensure that the court is notified*. If you are late, apologise unreservedly. To your professional client, lay client, opponent, and the court. Briefly explain the reason why you are late.

Let *both* your practice manager, *and* your instructing solicitor know that you have arrived, and keep them updated if there are any other complications.

If you need more time to have a conference before starting a hearing, inform the usher, and outline the reason why. Cases that are allocated to the small claims track are often listed together at 10:00 or 14:00. The court may be able to accommodate a request for more time by hearing another matter before the one that you are instructed in.

ii. Coats, umbrellas & bags

Advocates should not take unnecessary items (that are not necessary for the hearing) into court. One of the reasons for an advocates' room is so that legal representatives do not have to take coats, umbrellas, and bags into court. There is somewhere that these items can be left, *securely*.

If there is an advocates' room, and it is *lockable,* then, it should be used. Papers and electronic devices that contain confidential material, however, should *never* be left unattended. Even where there is the option of a locked room, it is safer to keep confidential material to hand.

iii. Disposal

Her Majesty's Courts and Tribunals Service ("HMCTS") met with the Bar Council to confirm the correct position as to who has responsibility for documents after hearings. In a joint notice, it was agreed that *only those documents (or bundles) belonging to legal representatives* should be removed by the legal representatives.

If they are not, and they contain 'special category (formerly sensitive) personal data', HMCTS 'may consider it necessary to report that a personal data breach has occurred pursuant to the General Data Protection Regulation and Data Protection Act 2018.' Documents that have been *filed* with the court should *not* be removed by *legal representatives*, however, as they are not data processors for the court.

iv. Correspondence

Whether you are corresponding with the court, professional client, or practice manager, you should follow appropriate *formalities*, be *prompt* in reverting, and *professional*.

1. Judge

As a general rule, *any* communication with the court on a matter of *substance* or *procedure must* be *disclosed* to, and *served* on, the other party (CPRs 27.2(1)(h) and 39.8). It is not only etiquette. It is a *rule of court*.

Usually, the legal representative representing the claimant, or an applicant making an application, will have "carriage" or the order. This means that they are responsible for three actions.

First, drafting it. Secondly, ensuring that it is an accurate reflection of the court's order, as prescribed in open court. Thirdly, handing the draft minute of order to the court's usher if it is handwritten, or emailing it to the court if it is electronic.

When corresponding with the court, via the judge's email address, the email should start "Dear Judge". It *must* state that it is being *copied* to the other party, her *identity*, and *capacity* (for example, solicitor). It should end with the title and surname of the legal representative sending the correspondence, and the party who they represent.

Do *not* copy in your *lay* client when corresponding with the court. Having sent the email, it can be forwarded to your *professional* client, so that they are aware of the date and time that the email was sent, content, and any attachments.

2. Ushers & other court staff

It is prudent to be courteous to ushers, and other court staff for four reasons.

First, and most importantly, they deserve it, as fellow human beings. Secondly, they speak to the judges. Thirdly, they are able to assist your case to be given more time before being called on, should you request it. Fourthly, if you would like a photocopy of an order, or you have forgotten to print out a vital document – although they are certainly not obliged – they may be more inclined to assist.

3. Professional client

Be courteous, revert promptly, and stick to deadlines. There is (so I am told) nothing a professional client hates more than counsel running late for a deadline. If there is potential for a problem to arise, do not put your head in the sand. Speak to your practice managers.

When a professional client instructs counsel, they are putting their neck on the line. They have an enormous stake in the case. If your professional client is unavailable, it may often be possible to take instructions from another member of her team.

4. Practice manager

There should be implicit trust and confidence between counsel and practice manager.

Counsel have to look after their practice manager's wellbeing, and vice versa. Demonstrate emotional intelligence, consideration, and flexibility. Doing so will give your practice manager confidence in corresponding with *you*, other *members* of chambers, and your *professional* clients.

b. Inside court

The key etiquette *in* court surrounds submissions, and encompasses ethics, in particular, criticism of other professionals. Remember that hearings are recorded.

i. Mobile telephones

There are three good reasons to keep a smart phone on silent.

First, to tether to your laptop, should the court not have a good wireless internet connection. Secondly, to use a calculator function, so as to work out damages, interest, and costs. Thirdly, to use a calendar function, so as to work out what the date is, for example, 21 days from the hearing.

ii. Entering & exiting

Wait for the names of the parties in your case to be called by the usher before moving to the door of the court in which your hearing will take place. As long as you have signed in, the matter will not go ahead without you, unless you have left the court building.

On entering and exiting court, it is etiquette to bow. In practice, this is a modest nod of the head, rather than a greeting that one imagines may be used when meeting the Queen. When exiting court, you should not leave the judge sitting in court with the other side. All parties should leave together. That may mean waiting for the other side.

Never, *ever* leave the judge with a *lay* individual.

Frequently, after the matter has concluded, the judge will say "good morning", or "good afternoon". It is normal to repeat the greeting. This is your cue that you may leave.

Alternatively, you may ask to be excused. This is very formal, however, and it may take some judge's by surprise, as you do not have to do so, and it is the same question that children ask in school. It may originate from the practice that you should not leave court before a judge has risen.

As such, another alternative is to enquire whether the court is rising. To this, most judges will understand that you are alluding to this custom, and say that they will stay in court, so that you may be excused.

iii. Seating

In general, most county court rooms are of an average, or perhaps slightly bigger than average size. Judges are not physically elevated, so that all court actors are at the same eye-level. Frequently, there are only three architectural features in-built into the court room, so as to convey that the judge is the decision-maker.

First, a royal crest above the judge. Secondly, a pronounced gap between where the parties sit, and where the judge sits. Thirdly, a vertical panel in front of the judge's desk, so that the parties cannot see what she is writing.

In other county courts, the rooms are larger, and the judge is sitting physically higher than the parties, so that the parties have to look up to catch the judge's eye. On occasion, in the County Court at Central London, judges sit in courtrooms used by the High Court, frequently, in the Queen's Building, or the West Green Building. If this is the case, it may be preferable to stand, so as to catch the judge's eye, and not to appear discourteous.

There are conventions surrounding where legal representatives, witnesses, and non-court actors are located in the courtroom. Much will depend on the layout, however, and, when a person is disabled, the courts usually permit that person to fulfil their role in the position that they are most comfortable in. If so, you can make the request on behalf of that person.

1. Parties

Legal representatives should sit at the front tables. Usually, the claimant sits on the left, and the defendant sits on the right, however, in some courts, this is reversed. If so, there will be signs on the respective tables, denominating which party is to sit at which table.

2. Witnesses

Witnesses (and the parties if they are represented) usually sit on the tables behind their legal representatives. When giving evidence, witnesses usually move to a table that is between that at which the parties sit, the judge, and off to one side. In absence of a separate, witness table, however, witnesses will sit at the table at which the legal representatives (or an unrepresented party) sit.

If so, the witness should only be able to see an *unmarked witness bundle*, as opposed to any (marked) documents that the parties are looking at. Care should be taken not to appear to give any visual cues, or otherwise project other body language when a witness is giving evidence. This can require more of a concerted effort where the witness is sitting next to you.

3. Non-court actors

Pupils and mini-pupils should sit at the back of the court, so that it is clear that they are not a legal representative, party, or witness. That is, they are not a court actor; they have no role in proceedings. They should be introduced before the hearing to the other party, and, at the start of the hearing for the court.

iv. Submissions

There are conventions surrounding how court actors are addressed, introducing the case, and how to react to an interruption. Do not make a positive submission unless you have instructions to do so, the evidence to support it, or, if it is a matter of law, you reasonably believe it to be correct. Be careful not knowingly to mislead the court by agreeing to a proposition of law to which you are not able to speak.

1. Forms of address

In the unlikely event that you are before a recorder, or a circuit judge, they should be referred to as "Your Honour". Deputy district judges, and full district judges should be referred to as "Sir" or "Madam".

Alternatively, judges can be referred to as "the court". This is preferable, as it is formal, and guards against the perception that you are over-familiar.

The convention is that counsel refer to one another as "my learned friend", and to a solicitor as "my friend". This can appear old-fashioned, and jarring, however, so many use title and surname instead.

Parties can be referred to by status, that is, claimant or defendant, or by their title and surname. Witnesses are referred to by their title and surname. Ushers are referred to as "Madam Usher" or "Mister Usher".

2. Introduction

As a general rule, it is safer to wait for the judge to invite you to speak before addressing the court. If the judge is writing when you enter court, she may be finalising the order of the previous matter. If in doubt, wait to be invited to speak.

Usually, the judge will introduce the case for the recording. You will have signed in with the usher, and sometimes case-management forms will have been completed before the hearing, on which the names of the parties, legal representatives, and witnesses are written. Accordingly, the judge is likely to state the names of the parties, case number, name of any advocate, and the parties that they represent before the hearing begins.

If the judge does not state the names of the advocates, it is etiquette to introduce the legal representative for the other side, using their title, surname, and stating the party that they represent. Introduce yourself, using your surname (and not your title), and state the party that you represent. If you have a person, who is not a court actor, but merely there to gain experience of the court process, introduce them, so that all court actors know who they are.

3. Interrupting

Do not interrupt another court actor, unless there is a *good* reason. Judge, counsel, or witness. If the judge, or another legal representative interrupts you, yield, and wait. If the interruption is unjustified, you will have the opportunity to explain the reason why, and the impact of doing so will not diminish having demonstrated that you are courteous.

An obvious exception is where a witness strays into relaying what she said to her counsel in the pre-hearing conference, and advice that her counsel gave, which are privileged.

4. Humility

If you cannot assist the court on a particular issue, say so.

Of course, you should do your best to acquire such knowledge of the facts and law, so as to understand what the respective cases are, facts that are in dispute, applicable law, and what you are inviting the court to do. But you must not mislead the court, knowingly, or *recklessly*. Better to show *reasonable* humility, and *appropriate* deference, than to invite, or otherwise to encourage the court to do something against the rules of court, or other authority, which is appealable.

5. Gestures

No matter your instinctive reaction to the evidence, submission, order, or judgment, try to retain your composure. When a witness is discourteous, let them be. It will undermine their evidence.

When a weak submission is made, the way to demonstrate it is through the evidence, and your submissions. If it is obviously weak, the judge may have already perceived it, without necessarily flagging it up, or requiring you to make verbose submissions on why it is weak.

Orders *will* be made, and judgments *will* be given, with which you do not agree. They are the *responsibility* of the *judge*. Not counsel, or solicitor. If it is arguably susceptible to an appeal, an application for permission to appeal can be made.

You are likely to be instructed in many more cases before *that* judge. You will be undermining your reputation with that judge, and perhaps also her colleagues, the usher, and court staff, if you visibly show your disapproval.

6. Criticism

Criticism should be *measured*, *reasoned*, and, unless there is a *good* reason, on *instructions*.

a. Experts

Criticism of experts, and their reports should be carefully considered, and, unless there is a good reason, only with explicit, written instructions. There may be an "expert" report on diminution in the value of a vehicle following a road traffic collision, for example, when there is no permission to rely on expert evidence, and the reasoning underpinning the conclusion does not withstand scrutiny.

If so, these points can be made in submissions, with reference to the court's directions, and the reasoning in the report, *without* attacking the expert *personally*. In a claim that is allocated to the small claims track, the author of an expert report is unlikely to attend the hearing, so as to respond to any criticism. Remember that the hearing is being recorded.

b. Legal representatives

Attacks on the conduct of a legal representative should also be *carefully* considered, and, unless there is a good reason, only made with *explicit*, written instructions. The conduct of those instructing is relevant for deciding what order to make as to costs. For example, in responding to requests for key documents, such as invoices, so as to narrow, and to potentially settle, the issues.

Where this can be identified ahead of the hearing, a *very* short witness statement from your professional client, setting out any non-compliance can assist. If appropriate, relevant correspondence should be exhibited, and, if necessary, *very* briefly explained.

If there is legitimate criticism to be made as to the manner in which a legal representative conducted litigation, it may also be possible expressly to state that no criticism is made of counsel at the hearing. If so, *say so*. Remember that the hearing is being recorded.

Appendix A
CPR 1.1 — The Overriding Objective

(1) These Rules are a new procedural code with the overriding objective of enabling the court to deal with cases justly and at proportionate cost.

(2) Dealing with a case justly and at proportionate cost includes, so far as is practicable—

   (a) ensuring that the parties are on an equal footing;

   (b) saving expense;

   (c) dealing with the case in ways which are proportionate—

      (i) to the amount of money involved;

      (ii) to the importance of the case;

      (iii) to the complexity of the issues; and

      (iv) to the financial position of each party;

   (d) ensuring that it is dealt with expeditiously and fairly;

   (e) allotting to it an appropriate share of the court's resources, while taking into account the need to allot resources to other cases; and

   (f) enforcing compliance with rules, practice directions and orders.

Appendix B
CPR 1.4 — Court's Duty To Manage Cases

(1) The court must further the overriding objective by actively managing cases.

(2) Active case management includes—

   (a) encouraging the parties to co-operate with each other in the conduct of the proceedings;

   (b) identifying the issues at an early stage;

   (c) deciding promptly which issues need full investigation and trial and accordingly disposing summarily of the others;

   (d) deciding the order in which issues are to be resolved;

   (e) encouraging the parties to use an alternative dispute resolution procedure if the court considers that appropriate and facilitating the use of such procedure;

   (f) helping the parties to settle the whole or part of the case;

   (g) fixing timetables or otherwise controlling the progress of the case;

   (h) considering whether the likely benefits of taking a particular step justify the cost of taking it;

   (i) dealing with as many aspects of the case as it can on the same occasion;

(j) dealing with the case without the parties needing to attend at court;

(k) making use of technology; and

(l) giving directions to ensure that the trial of a case proceeds quickly and efficiently.

Appendix C
Part 27 — The Small Claims Track

CPR 27.1 —Scope of this Part

(1) This Part—

    (a) sets out the special procedure for dealing with claims which have been allocated to the small claims track under Part 26; and

    (b) limits the amount of costs that can be recovered in respect of a claim which has been allocated to the small claims track.

    (Rule 27.14 deals with costs on the small claims track.)

(2) A claim being dealt with under this Part is called a small claim.

(Rule 26.6 provides for the scope of the small claims track. A claim for a remedy for harassment or unlawful eviction relating, in either case, to residential premises shall not be allocated to the small claims track whatever the financial value of the claim. Otherwise, the small claims track will be the normal track for—

- any claim which has a financial value of not more than £10,000 subject to the special provisions about claims for personal injuries and housing disrepair claims;

- any claim for personal injuries which has a financial value of not more than £10,000 where the claim for damages for personal injuries is not more than £1,000; and

- any claim which includes a claim by a tenant of residential premises against his landlord for repairs or other work to the premises where the estimated cost of the repairs or other work is not more than £1,000 and the financial value of any other claim for damages is not more than £1,000.)

CPR 27.2 —Extent to which other Parts apply

(1) The following Parts of these Rules do not apply to small claims—

(a) Part 25 (interim remedies) except as it relates to interim injunctions;

(b) Part 31 (disclosure and inspection);

(c) Part 32 (evidence) except rule 32.1 (power of court to control evidence);

(d) Part 33 (miscellaneous rules about evidence);

(e) Part 35 (experts and assessors) except rules 35.1 (duty to restrict expert evidence), 35.3 (experts—overriding duty to the court), 35.7 (court's power to direct that evidence is to be given by single joint expert) and 35.8 (instructions to a single joint expert);

(f) Subject to paragraph (3), Part 18 (further information);

(g) Part 36 (offers to settle); and

(h) Part 39 (hearings) except rule 39.2 (general rule—hearing to be in public) and rule 39.8 (communications with the court).

(2) The other Parts of these Rules apply to small claims except to the extent that a rule limits such application.

(3) The court of its own initiative may order a party to provide further information if it considers it appropriate to do so.

CPR 27.3 —Court's power to grant a final remedy

The court may grant any final remedy in relation to a small claim which it could grant if the proceedings were on the fast track or the multi-track.

CPR 27.4 —Preparation for the hearing

(1) After allocation the court will—

    (a) give standard directions and fix a date for the final hearing;

    (b) give special directions and fix a date for the final hearing;

    (c) give special directions and direct that the court will consider what further directions are to be given no later than 28 days after the date the special directions were given;

    (d) fix a date for a preliminary hearing under rule 27.6; or

    (e) give notice that it proposes to deal with the claim without a hearing under rule 27.10 and invite the parties to notify the court by a specified date if they agree the proposal.

(2) The court will—

(a) give parties at least 21 days' notice of the date fixed for the final hearing, unless the parties agree to accept less notice; and

(b) inform them of the amount of time allowed for the final hearing.

(3) In this rule—

(a) "standard directions" means—

(i) a direction that each party shall, at least 14 days before the date fixed for the final hearing, file and serve on every other party copies of all documents (including any expert's report) on which he intends to rely at the hearing; and

(ii) any other standard directions set out in Practice Direction 27; and

(b) "special directions" means directions given in addition to or instead of the standard directions.

CPR 27.5— Experts

No expert may give evidence, whether written or oral, at a hearing without the permission of the court.

CPR 27.6 —Preliminary hearing

(1) The court may hold a preliminary hearing for the consideration of the claim, but only—

(a) where—

(i) it considers that special directions, as defined in rule 27.4, are needed to ensure a fair hearing; and

(ii) it appears necessary for a party to attend at court to ensure that he understands what he must do to comply with the special directions; or

(b) to enable it to dispose of the claim on the basis that one or other of the parties has no real prospect of success at a final hearing; or

(c) to enable it to strike out a statement of case or part of a statement of case on the basis that the statement of case, or the part to be struck out, discloses no reasonable grounds for bringing or defending the claim.

(2) When considering whether or not to hold a preliminary hearing, the court must have regard to the desirability of limiting the expense to the parties of attending court.

(3) Where the court decides to hold a preliminary hearing, it will give the parties at least 14 days' notice of the date of the hearing.

(4) The court may treat the preliminary hearing as the final hearing of the claim if all the parties agree.

(5) At or after the preliminary hearing the court will—

(a) fix the date of the final hearing (if it has not been fixed already) and give the parties at least 21 days' notice of the date fixed unless the parties agree to accept less notice;

(b) inform them of the amount of time allowed for the final hearing; and

(c) give any appropriate directions.

CPR 27.7 —Power of court to add to, vary or revoke directions

The court may add to, vary or revoke directions.

CPR 27.8 —Conduct of the hearing

(1) The court may adopt any method of proceeding at a hearing that it considers to be fair.

(2) Hearings will be informal.

(3) The strict rules of evidence do not apply.

(4) The court need not take evidence on oath.

(5) The court may limit cross-examination.

(6) The court must give reasons for its decision.

CPR 27.9 —Non-attendance of parties at a final hearing

(1) If a party who does not attend a final hearing—

    (a) has given written notice to the court and the other party at least 7 days before the hearing date that he will not attend;

    (b) has served on the other party at least 7 days before the hearing date any other documents which he has filed with the court; and

    (c) has, in his written notice, requested the court to decide the claim in his absence and has confirmed his compliance with paragraphs (a) and (b) above, the court will take into account that party's statement of case and any other documents he has filed and served when it decides the claim.

(2) If a claimant does not—

    (a) attend the hearing; and

    (b) give the notice referred to in paragraph (1),

the court may strike out the claim.

(3) If—

    (a) a defendant does not—

        (i) attend the hearing; or

        (ii) give the notice referred to in paragraph (1); and

    (b) the claimant either—

        (i) does attend the hearing; or

        (ii) gives the notice referred to in paragraph (1),

    the court may decide the claim on the basis of the evidence of the claimant alone.

(4) If neither party attends or gives the notice referred to in paragraph (1), the court may strike out the claim and any defence and counterclaim.

CPR 27.10 —Disposal without a hearing

The court may, if all parties agree, deal with the claim without a hearing.

CPR 27.11 —Setting judgment aside and re-hearing

(1) A party—

    (a) who was neither present nor represented at the hearing of the claim; and

    (b) who has not given written notice to the court under rule 27.9(1),

may apply for an order that a judgment under this Part shall be set aside and the claim re-heard.

(2) A party who applies for an order setting aside a judgment under this rule must make the application not more than 14 days after the day on which notice of the judgment was served on him.

(3) The court may grant an application under paragraph (2) only if the applicant—

    (a) had a good reason for not attending or being represented at the hearing or giving written notice to the court under rule 27.9(1); and

    (b) has a reasonable prospect of success at the hearing.

(4) If a judgment is set aside —

    (a) the court must fix a new hearing for the claim; and

(b) the hearing may take place immediately after the hearing of the application to set the judgment aside and may be dealt with by the judge who set aside the judgment.

(5) A party may not apply to set aside a judgment under this rule if the court dealt with the claim without a hearing under rule 27.10.

(Rules 27.12 and 27.13 are revoked.)

CPR 27.14 —Costs on the small claims track

(1) This rule applies to any case which has been allocated to the small claims track.

(Rules 46.11 and 46.13 make provision in relation to orders for costs made before a claim has been allocated to the small claims track.)

(2) The court may not order a party to pay a sum to another party in respect of that other party's costs, fees and expenses, including those relating to an appeal, except—

(a) the fixed costs attributable to issuing the claim which—

(i) are payable under Part 45; or

(ii) would be payable under Part 45 if that Part applied to the claim;

(b) in proceedings which included a claim for an injunction or an order for specific performance a sum not exceeding the amount specified in Practice Direction 27 for legal advice and assistance relating to that claim;

(c) any court fees paid by that other party;

(d) expenses which a party or witness has reasonably incurred in travelling to and from a hearing or in staying away from home for the purposes of attending a hearing;

(e) a sum not exceeding the amount specified in Practice Direction 27 for any loss of earnings or loss of leave by a party or witness due to attending a hearing or to staying away from home for the purpose of attending a hearing;

(f) a sum not exceeding the amount specified in Practice Direction 27 for an expert's fees;

(g) such further costs as the court may assess by the summary procedure and order to be paid by a party who has behaved unreasonably;

(h) the Stage 1 and, where relevant, the Stage 2 fixed costs in rule 45.18 where—

   (i) the claim was within the scope of the Pre-Action Protocol for Low Value Personal Injury Claims in Road Traffic Accidents ("the RTA Protocol") or the Pre-action Protocol for Low Value Personal Injury (Employers' Liability and Public Liability) Claims ("the EL/PL Protocol");

   (ii) the claimant reasonably believed that the claim was valued at more than the small claims track limit in accordance with paragraph 4.1(4) of the relevant Protocol; and

   (iii) the defendant admitted liability under the process set out in the relevant Protocol; but

   (iv) the defendant did not pay those Stage 1 and, where relevant, Stage 2 fixed costs; and

(i) in an appeal, the cost of any approved transcript reasonably incurred.

(3) A party's rejection of an offer in settlement will not of itself constitute unreasonable behaviour under paragraph (2)(g) but the court may take it into consideration when it is applying the unreasonableness test.

(4) The limits on costs imposed by this rule also apply to any fee or reward for acting on behalf of a party to the proceedings charged by a person exercising a right of audience by virtue of an order under section 11 of the Courts and Legal Services Act 1990 (a lay representative).

CPR 27.15 —Claim re-allocated from the small claims track to another track

Where a claim is allocated to the small claims track and subsequently reallocated to another track, rule 27.14 (costs on the small claims track) will cease to apply after the claim has been re-allocated, and the fast track or multi-track costs rules will apply from the date of re-allocation.

Appendix D
Practice Direction 27 — Small Claims Track

Judges

[1] The functions of the court described in Part 27 which are to be carried out by a judge will generally be carried out by a District Judge but may be carried out by a Circuit Judge.

Case Management Directions

[2.1] Rule 27.4 explains how directions will be given, and rule 27.6 contains provisions about the holding of a preliminary hearing and the court's powers at such a hearing.

[2.2] Appendix A sets out details of the case that the court usually needs in the type of case described. Appendix B sets out the Standard Directions that the court may give. Appendix C sets out Special Directions that the court may give.

[2.3] Before allocating the claim to the Small Claims Track and giving directions for a hearing the court may require a party to give further information about that party's case.

[2.4] A party may ask the court to give particular directions about the conduct of the case.

[2.5] In deciding whether to make an order for exchange of witness statements the court will have regard to the following—

(a) whether either or both the parties are represented;

(b) the amount in dispute in the proceedings;

(c) the nature of the matters in dispute;

(d) whether the need for any party to clarify his case can better be dealt with by an order under paragraph 2.3;

(e) the need for the parties to have access to justice without undue formality, cost or delay.

Representation at a Hearing

[3.1] In this paragraph—

(1) a lawyer means a barrister, a solicitor or a legal executive employed by a solicitor or any other person authorised under the Legal Services Act 2007 to act as a litigator or advocate, and

(2) a lay representative means any other person.

[3.2]

(1) A party may present his own case at a hearing or a lawyer or lay representative may present it for him.

(2) The Lay Representatives (Right of Audience) Order 1999 provides that a lay representative may not exercise any right of audience—

(a) where his client does not attend the hearing;

(b) at any stage after judgment; or

(c) on any appeal brought against any decision made by the District Judge in the proceedings.

(3) However the court, exercising its general discretion to hear anybody, may hear a lay representative even in circumstances excluded by the Order.

(4) Any of its officers or employees may represent a corporate party.

Small Claim Hearing

[4.1] [Omitted.]

[4.2] A hearing that takes place at the court will generally be in the judge's room but it may take place in a courtroom.

[4.3] Rule 27.8 allows the court to adopt any method of proceeding that it considers to be fair and to limit cross-examination. The judge may in particular—

(1) ask questions of any witness himself before allowing any other person to do so,

(2) ask questions of all or any of the witnesses himself before allowing any other person to ask questions of any witnesses,

(3) refuse to allow cross-examination of any witness until all the witnesses have given evidence in chief,

(4) limit cross-examination of a witness to a fixed time or to a particular subject or issue, or both.

Recording Evidence and the Giving of Reasons

[5.1] A hearing that takes place at the court will be tape recorded by the court. A party may obtain a transcript of such a recording on payment of the proper transcriber's charges.

[5.2] Attention is drawn to section 9 of the Contempt of Court Act 1981 (which deals with the unauthorised use of tape recorders in court) and to the Practice Direction ([1981] 1 W.L.R. 1526) which relates to it.

[5.3]

(1) The judge may give reasons for his judgment as briefly and simply as the nature of the case allows.

(2) He will normally do so orally at the hearing, but he may give them later at a hearing either orally or in writing.

[5.4] Where the judge decides the case without a hearing under rule 27.10 or a party who has given notice under rule 27.9(1) does not attend the hearing, the judge will prepare a note of his reasons and the court will send a copy to each party.

[5.5] Nothing in this practice direction affects the duty of a judge at the request of a party to make a note of the matters referred to in section 80 of the County Courts Act 1984.

Non-attendance of a Party at a Hearing

[6.1] Attention is drawn to rule 27.9 (which enables a party to give notice that he will not attend a final hearing and sets out the effect of his giving such notice and of not doing so), and to paragraph 3 above.

[6.2] Nothing in those provisions affects the general power of the court to adjourn a hearing, for example where a party who wishes to attend a hearing on the date fixed cannot do so for a good reason.

Costs

[7.1] Attention is drawn to rule 27.14 which contains provisions about the costs which may be ordered to be paid by one party to another.

[7.2] The amount which a party may be ordered to pay under rule 27.14(2)(b) (for legal advice and assistance in claims including an injunction or specific performance) is a sum not exceeding £260.

[7.3] The amounts which a party may be ordered to pay under rule 27.14(3)(c) (loss of earnings) and (d) (experts' fees) are—

 (1) for the loss of earnings or loss of leave of each party or witness due to attending a hearing or staying away from home for the purpose of attending a hearing, a sum not exceeding £95 per day for each person, and

 (2) for experts' fees, a sum not exceeding £750 for each expert.

(As to recovery of pre-allocation costs in a case in which an admission by the defendant has reduced the amount in dispute to a figure below £10,000, reference should be made to paragraph 7.4 of Practice Direction 26 and to paragraph 7.1(3) of Practice Direction 46.)

Appeals

[8.1] Part 52 deals with appeals and attention is drawn to that Part and Practice Direction 52.

[8A] An appellant's notice in small claims must be filed and served in Form N164.

[8.2] Where the court dealt with the claim to which the appellant is a party—

(1) under rule 27.10 without a hearing; or

(2) in his absence because he gave notice under rule 27.9 requesting the court to decide the claim in his absence,

an application for permission to appeal must be made to the appeal court.

[8.3] Where an appeal is allowed the appeal court will, if possible, dispose of the case at the same time without referring the claim to the lower court or ordering a new hearing. It may do so without hearing further evidence.

Appendix A — Information and Documentation the Court Usually Needs in Particular Types of Case

ROAD ACCIDENT CASES (where the information or documentation is available)

- witness statements (including statements from the parties themselves);
- invoices and estimates for repairs;
- agreements and invoices for any car hire costs;
- the Police accident report;
- sketch plan which should wherever possible be agreed;
- photographs of the scene of the accident and of the damage.

BUILDING DISPUTES, REPAIRS, GOODS SOLD AND SIMILAR CONTRACTUAL CLAIMS (where the information or documentation is available)

- any written contract;
- photographs;
- any plans;
- a list of works complained of;
- a list of any outstanding works;
- any relevant estimate, invoice or receipt including any relating to repairs to each of the defects;
- invoices for work done or goods supplied;
- estimates for work to be completed;
- a valuation of work done to date.

LANDLORD AND TENANT CLAIMS (where the information or documentation is available)

- a calculation of the amount of any rent alleged to be owing, showing amounts received;
- details of breaches of an agreement which are said to justify withholding any deposit itemised showing how the total is made up and with invoices and estimates to support them.

BREACH OF DUTY CASES (negligence, deficient professional services and the like)

Details of the following:

- what it is said by the claimant was done negligently by the defendant;
- why it is said that the negligence is the fault of the defendant;

- what damage is said to have been caused;
- what injury or losses have been suffered and how any (and each) sum claimed has been calculated;
- the response of the defendant to each of the above.

Appendix B — Standard Directions

(For use where the District Judge specifies no other directions)

The Court Directs:

1. Each party must deliver to every other party and to the court office copies of all documents on which he intends to rely at the hearing no later than [..........] [14 days before the hearing]. (These should include the letter making the claim and the reply.)

2. The original documents must be brought to the hearing.

3. [Notice of hearing date and time allowed.]

4. The parties are encouraged to contact each other with a view to trying to settle the case or narrow the issues. However the court must be informed immediately if the case is settled by agreement before the hearing date.

5. No party may rely at the hearing on any report from an expert unless express permission has been granted by the court beforehand. Anyone wishing to rely on an expert must write to the court immediately on receipt of this Order and seek permission, giving an explanation why the assistance of an expert is necessary.

NOTE: Failure to comply with the directions may result in the case being adjourned and in the party at fault having to pay costs. The parties are encouraged always to try to settle the case by negotiating with each other. The court must be informed immediately if the case is settled before the hearing.

Appendix C — Special Directions

The .... must clarify his case.

He must do this by delivering to the court office and to the .... no later than ....

[a list of ....]

[details of ....]

The .... must allow the .... to inspect by appointment within ... days of receiving a request to do so.

The hearing will not take place at the court but at ....

The .... must bring to court at the hearing the ....

Signed statements setting out the evidence of all witnesses on whom each party intends to rely must be prepared and copies included in the documents mentioned in paragraph 1. This includes the evidence of the parties themselves and of any other witness, whether or not he is going to come to court to give evidence.

The court may decide not to take into account a document [or video] or the evidence of a witness if these directions have not been complied with.

If he does not [do so] [...] his [Claim] [Defence] [and Counterclaim] will be struck out and (specify consequence).

It appears to the court that expert evidence is necessary on the issue of ....and that that evidence should be given by a single expert to be instructed by the parties jointly. If the parties cannot agree about who to choose and what arrangements to make about paying his fee, either party MUST apply to the court for further directions. The evidence is to be given in the form of a written report. Either party may ask the expert questions and must then send copies of the questions and replies to the other party and to the court. Oral expert evidence may be allowed in exceptional circumstances but only after a further order of the court. Attention is drawn to the limit of £200 on expert's fees that may be recovered.

If either party intends to show a video as evidence he must—

(a) contact the court at once to make arrangements for him to do so, because the court may not have the necessary equipment, and

(b) provide the other party with a copy of the video or the opportunity to see it at least … days before the hearing.

Appendix E
Practice Direction —
Pre-Action Conduct and Protocols

Introduction

[1] Pre-action protocols explain the conduct and set out the steps the court would normally expect parties to take before commencing proceedings for particular types of civil claims. They are approved by the Master of the Rolls and are appendixed to the Civil Procedure Rules (CPR). (The current pre-action protocols are listed in paragraph 18.)

[2] This Practice Direction applies to disputes where no pre-action protocol approved by the Master of the Rolls applies.

Objectives of Pre-Action Conduct and Protocols

[3] Before commencing proceedings, the court will expect the parties to have exchanged sufficient information to—

(a) understand each other's position;

(b) make decisions about how to proceed;

(c) try to settle the issues without proceedings;

(d) consider a form of Alternative Dispute Resolution (ADR) to assist with settlement;

(e) support the efficient management of those proceedings; and

(f) reduce the costs of resolving the dispute.

Proportionality

[4] A pre-action protocol or this Practice Direction must not be used by a party as a tactical device to secure an unfair advantage over another party. Only reasonable and proportionate steps should be taken by the parties to identify, narrow and resolve the legal, factual or expert issues.

[5] The costs incurred in complying with a pre-action protocol or this Practice Direction should be proportionate (CPR 44.3(5)). Where parties incur disproportionate costs in complying with any pre-action protocol or this Practice Direction, those costs will not be recoverable as part of the costs of the proceedings.

Steps Before Issuing a Claim at Court

[6] Where there is a relevant pre–action protocol, the parties should comply with that protocol before commencing proceedings. Where there is no relevant pre-action protocol, the parties should exchange correspondence and information to comply with the objectives in paragraph 3, bearing in mind that compliance should be proportionate. The steps will usually include—

   (a) the claimant writing to the defendant with concise details of the claim. The letter should include the basis on which the claim is made, a summary of the facts, what the claimant wants from the defendant, and if money, how the amount is calculated;

   (b) the defendant responding within a reasonable time—14 days in a straight forward case and no more than 3 months in a very complex one. The reply should include confirmation as to whether the claim is accepted and, if it is not accepted, the reasons why, together with an explanation as to which facts and parts of the claim are disputed and whether the defendant is making a counterclaim as well as providing details of any counterclaim; and

(c) the parties disclosing key documents relevant to the issues in dispute.

Experts

[7] Parties should be aware that the court must give permission before expert evidence can be relied upon (see CPR 35.4(1)) and that the court may limit the fees recoverable. Many disputes can be resolved without expert advice or evidence. If it is necessary to obtain expert evidence, particularly in low value claims, the parties should consider using a single expert, jointly instructed by the parties, with the costs shared equally.

Settlement and ADR

[8] Litigation should be a last resort. As part of a relevant pre-action protocol or this Practice Direction, the parties should consider whether negotiation or some other form of ADR might enable them to settle their dispute without commencing proceedings.

[9] Parties should continue to consider the possibility of reaching a settlement at all times, including after proceedings have been started. Part 36 offers may be made before proceedings are issued.

[10] Parties may negotiate to settle a dispute or may use a form of ADR including—

(a) mediation, a third party facilitating a resolution;

(b) arbitration, a third party deciding the dispute;

(c) early neutral evaluation, a third party giving an informed opinion on the dispute; and

(d) Ombudsmen schemes.

(Information on mediation and other forms of ADR is available in the Jackson ADR Handbook (available from Oxford University Press) or at—

- http://www.civilmediation.justice.gov.uk/

- http://www.adviceguide.org.uk/england/law_e/ law_legal system_e/law taking legal_action_e/ alternatives_to_court.htm)

[11] If proceedings are issued, the parties may be required by the court to provide evidence that ADR has been considered. A party's silence in response to an invitation to participate or a refusal to participate in ADR might be considered unreasonable by the court and could lead to the court ordering that party to pay additional court costs.

Stocktake and List of Issues

[12] Where a dispute has not been resolved after the parties have followed a pre-action protocol or this Practice Direction, they should review their respective positions. They should consider the papers and the evidence to see if proceedings can be avoided and at least seek to narrow the issues in dispute before the claimant issues proceedings.

Compliance with this Practice Direction and the Protocols

[13] If a dispute proceeds to litigation, the court will expect the parties to have complied with a relevant pre-action protocol or this

Practice Direction. The court will take into account non-compliance when giving directions for the management of proceedings (see CPR 3.1(4) to (6)) and when making orders for costs (see CPR 44.3(5)(a)). The court will consider whether all parties have complied in substance with the terms of the relevant pre-action protocol or this Practice Direction and is not likely to be concerned with minor or technical infringements, especially when the matter is urgent (for example an application for an injunction).

[14] The court may decide that there has been a failure of compliance when a party has—

   (a) not provided sufficient information to enable the objectives in paragraph 3 to be met;

   (b) not acted within a time limit set out in a relevant protocol, or within a reasonable period; or

   (c) unreasonably refused to use a form of ADR, or failed to respond at all to an invitation to do so.

[15] Where there has been non-compliance with a pre-action protocol or this Practice Direction, the court may order that:

   (a) the parties are relieved of the obligation to comply or further comply with the pre-action protocol or this Practice Direction;

   (b) the proceedings are stayed while particular steps are taken to comply with the pre-action protocol or this Practice Direction;

   (c) sanctions are to be applied.

[16] The court will consider the effect of any non-compliance when deciding whether to impose any sanctions which may include—

(a) an order that the party at fault pays the costs of the proceedings, or part of the costs of the other party or parties;

(b) an order that the party at fault pay those costs on an indemnity basis;

(c) if the party at fault is a claimant who has been awarded a sum of money, an order depriving that party of interest on that sum for a specified period, and/or awarding interest at a lower rate than would otherwise have been awarded;

(d) if the party at fault is a defendant, and the claimant has been awarded a sum of money, an order awarding interest on that sum for a specified period at a higher rate, (not exceeding 10% above base rate), than the rate which would otherwise have been awarded.

Limitation

[17] This Practice Direction and the pre-action protocols do not alter the statutory time limits for starting court proceedings. If a claim is issued after the relevant limitation period has expired, the defendant will be entitled to use that as a defence to the claim. If proceedings are started to comply with the statutory time limit before the parties have followed the procedures in this Practice Direction or the relevant pre-action protocol, the parties should apply to the court for a stay of the proceedings while they so comply.

Protocols in Force

[18] The table sets out the protocols currently in force and from which date.

PROTOCOL	CAME INTO FORCE
Personal Injury	6 April 2015
Resolution of Clinical Disputes	6 April 2015
Construction and Engineering	02 October 2000
Defamation	02 October 2000
Professional Negligence	16 July 2000
Judicial Review	6 April 2015
Disease and Illness	8 December 2003
Housing Disrepair	6 April 2015
Possession Claims by Social Landlords	6 April 2015
Possession Claims for Mortgage Arrears	6 April 2015
Dilapidation of Commercial Property	1 January 2012
Low Value Personal Injury Road Traffic Accident Claims	30 April 2010 extended from 31 July 2013
Low Value Personal Injury Employers' and Public Liability Claims	31 July 2013
Debt Claims	1 October 2017
Resolution of Package Travel Claims	7 May 2018

Pre-Action Conduct Practice Direction (para.9.3, amended 1 October 2009, as reproduced from Civil Procedure 2013)

[9.3] Information about funding arrangements

Where a party enters into a funding arrangement within the meaning of rule 43.2(1)(k), that party must inform the other parties about this arrangement as soon as possible and in any event either within 7 days of entering into the funding arrangement concerned or, where a claimant enters into a funding arrangement before sending a letter before claim, in the letter before claim.

(CPR rule 44.3B(1)(c) provides that a party may not recover certain additional costs where information about a funding arrangement was not provided.)

MORE BOOKS BY LAW BRIEF PUBLISHING

A selection of our other titles available now:-

'Ellis on Credit Hire – Sixth Edition' by Aidan Ellis & Tim Kevan
'Tackling Disclosure in the Criminal Courts – A Practitioner's Guide' by Narita Bahra QC & Don Ramble
'A Practical Guide to TOLATA Claims' by Greg Williams
'Artificial Intelligence – The Practical Legal Issues' by John Buyers
'A Practical Guide to Prison Injury Claims' by Malcolm Johnson
'A Practical Guide to Hackney Carriage Licensing in London' by Stuart Jessop
'A Practical Guide to Advising Clients at the Police Station' by Colin Stephen McKeown-Beaumont
'A Practical Guide to Antisocial Behaviour Injunctions' by Iain Wightwick
'Practical Mediation: A Guide for Mediators, Advocates, Advisers, Lawyers, and Students in Civil, Commercial, Business, Property, Workplace, and Employment Cases' by Jonathan Dingle with John Sephton
'Planning Obligations Demystified: A Practical Guide to Planning Obligations and Section 106 Agreements' by Bob Mc Geady & Meyric Lewis
'A Practical Guide to Crofting Law' by Brian Inkster
'A Practical Guide to Spousal Maintenance' by Liz Cowell
'A Practical Guide to the Law of Domain Names and Cybersquatting' by Andrew Clemson
'A Practical Guide to the Law of Gender Pay Gap Reporting' by Harini Iyengar
'A Practical Guide to the Rights of Grandparents in Children Proceedings' by Stuart Barlow
'NHS Whistleblowing and the Law' by Joseph England
'Employment Law and the Gig Economy' by Nigel Mackay & Annie Powell
'A Practical Guide to the General Data Protection Regulation (GDPR)' by Keith Markham

- 'A Practical Guide to Noise Induced Hearing Loss (NIHL) Claims' by Andrew Mckie, Ian Skeate, Gareth McAloon
- 'An Introduction to Beauty Negligence Claims – A Practical Guide for the Personal Injury Practitioner' by Greg Almond
- 'Intercompany Agreements for Transfer Pricing Compliance' by Paul Sutton
- 'Zen and the Art of Mediation' by Martin Plowman
- 'A Practical Guide to the SRA Principles, Individual and Law Firm Codes of Conduct 2019 – What Every Law Firm Needs to Know' by Paul Bennett
- 'A Practical Guide to Licensing Law for Commercial Property Lawyers' by Niall McCann & Richard Williams
- 'A Practical Guide to Adoption for Family Lawyers' by Graham Pegg
- 'Essential Motor Finance Law for the Busy Practitioner' by Richard Humphreys
- 'A Practical Guide to Industrial Disease Claims' by Andrew Mckie & Ian Skeate
- 'A Practical Guide to the Law of Armed Conflict' by Jo Morris & Libby Anderson
- 'A Practical Guide to Redundancy' by Philip Hyland
- 'A Practical Guide to Vicarious Liability' by Mariel Irvine
- 'A Practical Guide to Claims Arising from Delays in Diagnosing Cancer' by Bella Webb
- 'A Practical Guide to Applications for Landlord's Consent and Variation of Leases' by Mark Shelton
- 'A Practical Guide to Relief from Sanctions Post-Mitchell and Denton' by Peter Causton
- 'Butler's Equine Tax Planning: 2nd Edition' by Julie Butler
- 'A Practical Guide to Equity Release for Advisors' by Paul Sams
- 'A Practical Guide to Unlawful Eviction and Harassment' by Stephanie Lovegrove
- 'A Practical Guide to the Law Relating to Food' by Ian Thomas
- 'A Practical Guide to the Ending of Assured Shorthold Tenancies' by Elizabeth Dwomoh
- 'A Practical Guide to Financial Services Claims' by Chris Hegarty
- 'The Law of Houses in Multiple Occupation: A Practical Guide to HMO Proceedings' by Julian Hunt
- 'A Practical Guide to Unlawful Eviction and Harassment' by Stephanie Lovegrove

'A Practical Guide to Solicitor and Client Costs' by Robin Dunne
'A Practical Guide to Wrongful Conception, Wrongful Birth and Wrongful Life Claims' by Rebecca Greenstreet
'Occupiers, Highways and Defective Premises Claims: A Practical Guide Post-Jackson – 2nd Edition' by Andrew Mckie
'A Practical Guide to Financial Ombudsman Service Claims' by Adam Temple & Robert Scrivenor
'A Practical Guide to the Law of Enfranchisement and Lease Extension' by Paul Sams
'A Practical Guide to Marketing for Lawyers – 2nd Edition' by Catherine Bailey & Jennet Ingram
'A Practical Guide to Advising Schools on Employment Law' by Jonathan Holden
'Certificates of Lawful Use and Development: A Guide to Making and Determining Applications' by Bob Mc Geady & Meyric Lewis
'A Practical Guide to the Law of Dilapidations' by Mark Shelton
'A Guide to Consent in Clinical Negligence Post-Montgomery' by Lauren Sutherland QC
'A Practical Guide to Running Housing Disrepair and Cavity Wall Claims: 2nd Edition' by Andrew Mckie & Ian Skeate
'A Practical Guide to Digital and Social Media Law for Lawyers' by Sherree Westell
'A Practical Guide to Holiday Sickness Claims – 2nd Edition' by Andrew Mckie & Ian Skeate
'A Practical Guide to Elderly Law' by Justin Patten
'Arguments and Tactics for Personal Injury and Clinical Negligence Claims' by Dorian Williams
'A Practical Guide to QOCS and Fundamental Dishonesty' by James Bentley
'A Practical Guide to Drone Law' by Rufus Ballaster, Andrew Firman, Eleanor Clot
'A Practical Guide to Compliance for Personal Injury Firms Working With Claims Management Companies' by Paul Bennett
'A Practical Guide to the Landlord and Tenant Act 1954: Commercial Tenancies' by Richard Hayes & David Sawtell
'A Practical Guide to Psychiatric Claims in Personal Injury' by Liam Ryan
'A Practical Guide to Dog Law for Owners and Others' by Andrea Pitt

'RTA Allegations of Fraud in a Post-Jackson Era: The Handbook – 2nd Edition' by Andrew Mckie
'RTA Personal Injury Claims: A Practical Guide Post-Jackson' by Andrew Mckie
'On Experts: CPR35 for Lawyers and Experts' by David Boyle
'An Introduction to Personal Injury Law' by David Boyle
'A Practical Guide to Claims Arising From Accidents Abroad and Travel Claims' by Andrew Mckie & Ian Skeate
'A Practical Guide to Chronic Pain Claims' by Pankaj Madan
'A Practical Guide to Claims Arising from Fatal Accidents' by James Patience
'A Practical Approach to Clinical Negligence Post-Jackson' by Geoffrey Simpson-Scott
'Employers' Liability Claims: A Practical Guide Post-Jackson' by Andrew Mckie
'A Practical Guide to Subtle Brain Injury Claims' by Pankaj Madan
'A Practical Guide to Costs in Personal Injury Cases' by Matthew Hoe
'The No Nonsense Solicitors' Practice: A Guide To Running Your Firm' by Bettina Brueggemann
'The Queen's Counsel Lawyer's Omnibus: 20 Years of Cartoons from The Times 1993-2013' by Alex Steuart Williams

These books and more are available to order online direct from the publisher at www.lawbriefpublishing.com, where you can also read free sample chapters. For any queries, contact us on 0844 587 2383 or mail@lawbriefpublishing.com.

Our books are also usually in stock at www.amazon.co.uk with free next day delivery for Prime members, and at good legal bookshops such as Wildy & Sons.

We are regularly launching new books in our series of practical day-to-day practitioners' guides. Visit our website and join our free newsletter to be kept informed and to receive special offers, free chapters, etc.

You can also follow us on Twitter at www.twitter.com/lawbriefpub.

Printed in Great Britain
by Amazon